Chalk landscape: the scarp slope of the Berkshire Downs.

Shire County Guide 34

BERKSHIRE

Peter Speed

Shire Publications Ltd

CONTENTS

Printed in Great Britain by C. I. Thomas & Sons (Haverfordwest) Ltd, Press Buildings, Merlins Bridge, Haverfordwest, Dyfed SA61 1XF.

British Library Cataloguing in Publication Data: Speed, P. F. (Peter Frederick). Berkshire. I. Title. 914.22904858. ISBN 0-7478-0148-7.

ACKNOWLEDGEMENTS
The author and publishers gratefully acknowledge the assistance of Mr Tony Higgott, Curator, Newbury District Museum, in the preparation of this book and also of the following: Mr Martin Brown, Recreation Development Officer (East), British Waterways; Mr J. Cannon, Domestic Bursar, Bearwood College; Mr Phillip Chesterton; Mr C. L. Cram, Reading Museum and Art Gallery; Mr Paul Quarrie, Librarian, Eton College. Photographs are acknowledged as follows: Courage Shire Horse Centre, page 40; Dorney Court, page 32; Cadbury Lamb, pages 26 (top), 28 (left), 38, 43, 44, 55, 64, 66 (lower), 73 (both), 74 and 76 (both); Royalty and Empire, Windsor Station Limited, page 42. The cover and remaining photographs are by the author. The maps and plans are by Robert Dizon.

NOTE
The locations of many of the places described in this book are identified by means of the national grid reference, given in the form of the two grid letters (denoting the 100 km square) and six figures, locating the site to within 100 metres. Each reference is preceded by the number of the Ordnance Survey (OS) Landranger map on which the place will be found: for example, OS 174: SU 414707. A full explanation of how to use grid references may be found on Landranger maps.

Cover: *The Thames at Streatley.*

Below: *Sheep in clover: on the Downs, near Compton.*

'Prairie farming': on the Downs, near Lambourn.

1
The making of Berkshire

History

It has been said that when people have not been fighting in Berkshire, they have been hurrying through it to reach other destinations. Such a remark is most unfair, but it is indeed true that a great deal of the history of the county is about conflicts and communications.

Stone age, bronze age and iron age people all lived in this area and left their mark on the landscape. There are burial mounds from the new stone age onwards, iron age hillforts and, most impressive of all, trackways. Two important prehistoric thoroughfares follow the rims of the London Basin, Old Way to the south and the Ridgeway to the north. While Old Way is only in Berkshire for a short distance, the Ridgeway runs the length of the Downs, although much of what was in Berkshire was transferred to Oxfordshire in 1974. It is a splendid place to walk, with spectacular views.

After their invasion of AD 43 the Romans built one of their towns, *Calleva Atrebatum*, just south of the county boundary. There were several roads radiating from it, including one later known as the Devil's Highway, which ran to London.

After the fall of the Roman Empire, Berkshire became a cockpit. First, the Saxons took it from the Romano-Britons in the sixth century; then two Saxon kingdoms, Mercia and Wessex, fought over it and, finally, the Danish Vikings raided it several times, beginning in AD 871.

As in the rest of England, the Normans made sure that every parish had a church and many a Berkshire church still contains some of their work. Also, William the Conqueror built Windsor Castle. To him, it was just one fortress in a ring which he put round London, but it became the most important royal castle in England, a royal palace and a unique religious foundation.

From the middle ages to the seventeenth century, the wool and cloth trade was important in Berkshire, though, to judge from the churches, it brought less wealth to this part of England than to the Cotswolds and East Anglia. St Nicolas's, Newbury, is Berkshire's only 'wool church', owing its magnificence to a wealthy cloth merchant.

The armies of both Royalists and Parliamentarians came and went in Berkshire during the Civil War, and there were two battles, both near Newbury. They were important

Eocene landscape, near Thatcham.

engagements, with heavy casualties, though neither was as decisive as Marston Moor or Naseby.

Berkshire farmers played a leading part in the agricultural revolution of the eighteenth and early nineteenth centuries. One of its pioneers, Jethro Tull, carried out his trials at Prosperous Farm, just south of Hungerford. But while farmers and landowners thrived, farm labourers did not. They took part in the Swing Riots of 1830, breaking threshing machines, burning ricks and ducking unpopular overseers of the poor in ponds. The Berkshire authoress Mary Russell Mitford wrote a vivid account of these events in her marvellous book *Our Village*.

Also during the eighteenth and early nineteenth centuries, there were important changes in transport. The Bath Road, which had been little better than a series of rough tracks, was improved by turnpike trusts. Coaching inns flourished along the route, some modest, others no:

The famous inn at Speenhamland that
    stands below the hill
May well be called the Pelican from its
    enormous bill.

The Pelican is no more, but many inns, like the Bear at Hungerford, have survived. Also, west of Newbury, is the hamlet of Halfway, so called because that is its position between London and Bath.

Waterways were important. The Thames was improved for navigation; the Kennet had been canalised between Reading and Newbury by 1723 and the Kennet and Avon Canal opened in 1810, joining Bath and Newbury.

Brunel's Great Western Railway was completed as far as Bristol in 1841 and then branch lines were built. The railways were a doubtful blessing for Berkshire, since they drained the best people from the west of the county. However, the east was now within easy reach of London. James Morrison, the owner of Basildon Park, was pleased that he could live at home and work in London, 'thanks to Brunel and forty miles an hour'. Londoners settled in east Berkshire, taking advantage of the cheap land and the gravel soils, which they believed were healthy. Institutions followed, like Wellington College and Broadmoor.

The industrial revolution of the nineteenth century was based on coal and made little difference to Berkshire, only Reading growing to any size. The industrial revolution of the twentieth century, though, was based on electricity and has transformed the county, growth being even more rapid after the M4 motorway opened in 1974. Much of 'Silicon Valley' is in Berkshire. Here time is money and, judging by the way people drive, a very great deal of money.

Geology

The age of the earth is 4600 million years; chalk, the oldest visible rock in Berkshire, began forming a mere 100 million years ago. It was made from coccoliths, the armour of algae so minute that there could be a million of them in a litre of water. As the algae died, the coccoliths accumulated on the sea bed, where they compacted to form chalk. This went on for 30 million years, the chalk growing in depth at the rate of a millimetre every fifty years. Its total area is not known, but it certainly covered much of what is now southern England, the English Channel and northern France.

Chalk is 98 per cent pure calcium carbonate, and the only foreign bodies of any significance in it are flints. Chemically, these are silica, some of which came from the skeletons of sea creatures and some of which was deposited directly from the sea.

Eventually, owing to changes in land and sea level, the chalk emerged from the water. Then, during 50 million years, it was folded into ridges and troughs known as anticlines and synclines. It was also eroded, so that the anticlines have vanished, leaving only their ragged edges as low ranges of hills. Through the action of carbonic acid in rainwater, these too, are shrinking, at the rate of a millimetre every twenty years.

One of the chalk synclines is the London Basin. In plan it is, very roughly, the shape of a V lying on its side. The closed end is in the region of Marlborough, Wiltshire, while the open end vanishes into the North Sea. The ridge along the London Basin's northern boundary begins as the Berkshire Downs, then breaks where the Thames flows through the Goring Gap. It continues as the Chiltern Hills on the Buckinghamshire side of the river. The southern ridge is the Hampshire Downs, the Hog's Back and the North Downs.

Berkshire is towards the narrow end of the London Basin, so there is a great deal of chalk in the west of the county, including most of the Berkshire Downs. The Downs are a north-facing escarpment, which means they have a steep, or scarp, slope to the north and a gentler dip slope to the south. All the southern

Sand and gravel landscape: Wokefield Common.

ridge of the London Basin is outside Berkshire, save where a salient in the extreme south-west of the county reaches into the Hampshire Downs. Here, too, there is a north-facing escarpment and on it are Inkpen and Walbury Hills. At 974 feet (297 metres), Walbury is the highest chalk hill in England.

Even as the London Basin was forming, rivers flowed into it, while the sea invaded it from time to time. As a result, silt, sand, gravel and pebbles were laid on the chalk and are known as Eocene deposits. The silt has now become clay. In the order in which they were laid down, the Eocene deposits are the Reading Beds, London Clay and the Bagshot Beds.

Eocene deposits blanket the chalk in east Berkshire, though here and there folding has forced isolated hills through the cover. Windsor Castle stands on one of these hills. The Eocene continues into the west of the county but tapers away to nothing as the chalk ridges converge.

Most of the Bagshot Beds have been eroded, exposing large areas of London Clay, as for example at Windsor Great Park. Erosion has also removed many of the Eocene deposits from the lower slopes of the chalk, though residues of them may remain in the form of clay-with-flints. Also, in a few places on the chalk, there are sarsens. These are hard, sandstone boulders that may once have formed part of a continuous sheet, now broken and almost entirely lost.

During the ice ages, the last of which was 12,000 years ago, the ice sheet came no further south than the Thames, but melt-waters from it flooded over Berkshire, spreading pebbles and gravel. Where these deposits remain, they are known as Plateau Gravels.

The Thames is not only a major feature of the landscape but has done much to shape it. The river makes a dramatic entry through the Goring Gap, which breaks the chalk ridge. Probably the river was there first and, as the land rose, so it wore down its bed. Further east, the Thames also wore down its bed as the land rose, and at its former levels there are terraces, strewn with gravel. These are difficult for the untrained eye to spot, but the results of lateral erosion are clear to see. Lateral erosion happens when a river moves sideways, wearing away one bank and depositing silt on the other. The deposits make fertile land, almost perfectly level, as, for example, around Cookham. If the erosion takes away

the foot of a hill, then there may be a slope which is almost a precipice. The Buckinghamshire bank of the Cliveden reach, between Maidenhead and Cookham, is one example, and so is the north side of the hill on which Windsor Castle stands.

Landscapes

Berkshire's varied geology has produced varied landscapes. The tops of the chalk downs are open rolling country with occasional clumps of trees, mainly beech. These areas are good for sheep rearing and their soils are easy to cultivate. The lower slopes of the chalk are covered with clay-with-flints, which, though full of stones, is fertile.

Left to nature, the Eocene clays would be covered with broad-leaved trees. Cleared for farming, they produce an abundance of grass, which is good for cattle.

The gravels and many of the sands are too barren to be worth cultivating. Until the twentieth century villagers used them as commons, where they sent their animals for such grazing as they could find. This created open heathland as trees were unable to grow. Now that the grazing has ceased, many of these areas have been invaded by pine, birch and bracken, though they are still known as commons, as for example Bucklebury Common.

Building materials

The geology of Berkshire is seen in its older buildings. Unfortunately chalk, the most common rock, weathers easily, though some of it is hard enough to be used inside. The columns of Enborne church are made from it. Chalk is also easy to carve, there being some particularly beautiful work in Warfield church.

Sarsens have the opposite qualities to chalk, for they are durable but difficult to shape. They have been used where appearance is not too important, for example in humbler buildings and in the walls of Windsor Castle.

Flints are very durable and are found in buildings everywhere in the county, but they cannot be used on their own. Often they are used in conjunction with bricks. Freestone, such as Bath stone or Portland stone, has also been used for quoins, door and window surrounds and window tracery. Berkshire, however, has no freestone, so any needed in the county had to be brought there at great expense and builders used it as economically as possible. The only important secular building which is entirely in freestone and earlier than 1800 is Basildon Park. After the Kennet and Avon Canal opened in 1810, it carried a certain amount of Bath stone. Hungerford church and the Royal Berkshire Hospital at Reading were built from it.

Berkshire has plenty of clay and as oak trees flourished on it many older houses are timber-framed. Numbers of churches have wooden bellcotes covered with shingles.

Much of Berkshire's clay is suitable for making bricks, which were used in this county earlier than in much of England. Some of the brickwork in Eton College, for example, dates from the 1440s. In the later middle ages many parishes that had done without church towers found they could afford them in brick. For houses, bricks were used both on their own and as infilling for timber frames.

Before the nineteenth century bricks were hand-made, so they were slightly irregular and therefore attractive. Sonning, which is full of brick and tile houses, beautifully mellowed, is as pleasant a village as any built of stone.

Bricks can be made in whatever shape is wanted and they come in different colours, so it is possible to produce all sorts of interesting effects with them. At first this was done with restraint, but the combined results of mass production and Victorian taste were, at times, startling. Street's church of All Saints at Boyn Hill, Maidenhead, shows the lengths to which a nineteenth-century architect would go in making patterns with bricks.

Population

Berkshire has a population of 700,000, though it is not spread evenly. Newbury District covers all the county west of Reading, an area of 273 square miles (707 sq km). The population is 130,000, giving a density of 476 to the square mile. The rest of the county covers 217 square miles (562 sq km), with a population of 570,000. This gives a density of 2628 to the square mile. The west of Berkshire, then, is largely rural, while the east is mainly urban. The east, though, is far from being a vast conurbation and the towns, with the exceptions of Slough and Bracknell, are attractive and interesting.

Today Berkshire is full of life, bustle and prosperity, while any programme of events will show that its people are highly educated, intelligent and dedicated to all manner of worthwhile activities.

Rural Berkshire: cricket match at West Ilsley.

The view from Lowbury Hill.

2
The countryside

Berkshire has much delightful countryside. There are walks of every grade of difficulty from gentle strolls along level towpaths to strenuous hikes over the downs. There are water activities of many kinds, such as travelling in a horse-drawn canal barge, fishing or windsurfing. There are many different habitats for wildlife, notably chalk downland, heathland, deciduous and coniferous woodlands, wetlands, rivers, streams, lakes and ponds.

Tourist information centres stock several useful publications about the countryside. The East Berkshire Ramblers' Association Group produces three books of walks, *Rambling for Pleasure in East Berkshire*, *Rambling for Pleasure around Reading* and *Rambling for Pleasure along the Thames*. The same association also produces eight footpath maps on the scale of 2½ inches to the mile. Helen and Michael Weideli have produced several books of walks under the title *On Foot in West Berks*. The County Council's Department of Highways and Planning produces a set of leaflets, *Countryside Walks and Rides*, which describes walks in many different places and varying in length from 2 to 6 miles (3-10 km). An indispensable book for anyone wishing to make a serious study of the wildlife of the area is *The Wildlife of the Thames Counties*, edited by Richard Fitter and produced by the Berkshire, Buckinghamshire and Oxfordshire Naturalists' Trust (BBONT). This may be obtained from the Trust's office at 3 Church Cowley Road, Rose Hill, Oxford OX4 3JR (telephone: 0865 775476). Another admirable book is *A Naturalist's Guide to the Wild Life of the Newbury District* published by Newbury Museum.

Bucklebury Common. Car parks at OS 174: SU 555692 and 561692. Open at all times. From A4 turn north in Woolhampton towards Bucklebury. Woolhampton is 6 miles (10 km) east of Newbury.

This is over 2 square miles (5 sq km) of mixed woodland with numerous paths. The inhabitants of Bucklebury claim there are 268 footpaths in their parish. On the edge of the common is the Blade Bone Inn (571697) and running east-northeast from here, along a minor road, is an avenue of oaks. The trees have been planted at various times to celebrate important events, supposedly beginning with a local visit by Elizabeth I in 1568, then the victories of the Duke of Marlborough, the battle of Trafalgar, and, most recently, a visit by Elizabeth II in 1972.

California Country Park, Nine Mile Ride, Finchampstead (OS 175: SU 787647). Telephone: 0734 730028. Take the minor road which is the continuation of B3430 from Bracknell.

This large and attractive park is run admirably by Wokingham District Council. It contains woods with 34 species of trees, a lake, a dragonfly pond and a bog that is an area of special scientific interest. There are organised walks to study different kinds of wildlife and for nature photography.

The park is a paradise for toddlers, with play areas and a huge paddling pool. From time to time there is a Teddy Bears' Picnic. On certain days rangers take children round the park and teach them about the countryside. Adults can play tennis, fish or just relax.

The park has an information centre.

Cock Marsh, north-west of Cookham. The marsh is best approached from the car park on Cookham Moor (OS 175: SU 894854). Open at all times.

The total area of the site is 132 acres (53 ha) and, as well as marshy land, there are steep chalk slopes. There are good flora of both habitats including, in the marshland, the water violet.

Cookham Moor is similar, but less rewarding.

Crowthorne Wood, south of Bracknell. The best approaches are from The Look Out (OS 175: SU 876661) or the car park on the Devil's Highway (OS 175: SU 844644). Open at all times.

There are danger areas to the south, because of the ranges at Sandhurst. Also, walkers should take a careful note of their route, because it is possible to get lost.

Crowthorne Wood is just part of an area of several square miles of woodland, mainly coniferous, growing on sandy soils that must once have supported nothing but heaths. Many miles of tracks criss-cross the woods, nine radiating from Lower Star Point alone (OS 175: SU 875640).

California Country Park.

Dinton Pastures Country Park, Davis Street, Hurst, Reading RG10 0TH. Telephone: 0734 342061. Entrance at OS 175: SU 785717.

Dinton Pastures Country Park covers many acres. Like California Country Park, it is run by Wokingham District Council and is just as excellent. There is an information centre.

Until the 1970s, the area covered by the park was being excavated for sand and gravel, but the former pits now make attractive lakes and ponds. There are, as well, a river, a stream, hedgerows and meadow. In these varied habitats all kinds of wildlife thrive, such as butterflies and other insects, mammals and many species of birds.

This is a pleasant place for casual visitors to stroll and picnic, but there are also plenty of organised activities. The Park Office will supply a list of these, free of charge. For young children there are Teddy Bears' Picnics and Activity Days. For children aged eight to fourteen there is an Action Countryside summer playground scheme.

One of the lakes has been stocked for coarse fishing and anyone with a rod and line licence may buy a day ticket. On the largest of the lakes there are canoeing and windsurfing. There is sailing, too, though visitors who want a day ticket must go to the Black Swan Sailing Club in Sandford Lane. This is less than a mile from the entrance to the country park, north along the B3030 (telephone: 0734 345116).

The Museum of Berkshire Aviation has a site in Dinton Pastures Country Park. When it is opened, this museum will be of great interest to anyone who is keen on aviation. The most important displays will be on Miles Aircraft, the Air Transport Auxiliary and the D-Day airborne operations.

Finchampstead Ridges, 3 miles (5 km) south of Wokingham. There is roadside parking at OS 175: SU 807635 and nearby is the Simon's Wood car park at 813635. Open at all times.

The 60 acres (24 ha) are covered with heather and woodland, mainly coniferous. From them are fine views across Berkshire, Hampshire and Surrey.

Hungerford Marsh, just north-west of Hungerford (OS 174: SU 333688). Go through Hungerford churchyard and follow the footpath which crosses the Kennet and Avon Canal. Open at all times.

This is a Site of Special Scientific Interest. In the 26 acres (11 ha) are reed beds, a stream and grassland, so there is a good variety of vegetation and wildlife. In all, 120 bird species have been recorded. Those that breed here are reed and sedge warblers, little grebes, coots and snipe. In summer there are yellow wagtails and grasshopper warblers; in winter there are siskins and all the year round there are kingfishers and grey wagtails.

Inkpen Beacon and Walbury Hill, 1½ miles (2.4 km) south of Inkpen village. There is parking at OS 174: SU 370620 and 379616. Follow the instructions to Inkpen Common (see below) and continue towards Combe.

These hills are on the edge of the chalk ridge which divides the Thames and Hampshire basins. There is good walking along the ridge to the east and the west, with splendid views.

There is a long barrow on Inkpen Hill on which stands a gibbet, in good order and ready for use. Keeping it in repair has been the condition of the lease of a local farmer. The gibbet was erected for a couple who committed murder, so it has a crossbar, giving a 'his' side and a 'hers'. (See also chapter 3.)

The Kennet and Avon Canal at Kintbury.

Inkpen Common, east of Inkpen village (OS 174: SU 382644). In Kintbury, turn south towards Inkpen. At the top of the hill is a crossroads with a cemetery beside it. Go straight on and then fork right. Stop at the next road junction, by the BBONT sign. Open at all times.

This is a Site of Special Scientific Interest. There are 26 acres (11 ha) of acid plateau gravel, lying on chalk. In the centre of the common is open heath with heather, gorse, acidic grassland and some birch and oak. Around the fringes are birch and some mature woodland. There is a wet valley bog and a pond has been made in an old clay pit to encourage aquatic life. There are numbers of plants which are unusual for Berkshire, such as dwarf gorse, lousewort, devil's-bit scabious, bog asphodel and petty whin. Birds breeding here include several species of warbler, tree pipits, yellowhammers, cuckoos and kestrels. There are numerous butterflies and spiders.

Kennet and Avon Canal
Both the canal and its banks are rich in wildlife. (See chapter 7.)

Lambourn Seven Barrows. This site is to the east of the minor road which runs from Lambourn to Kingston Lisle. There is parking a short distance down the track at OS 174: SU 329827. Open at all times.

These 3 acres (1.2 ha) of chalk grassland have never been ploughed and are not grazed, though they are carefully managed. Over a hundred species of plants have been found here and there are many butterflies. (See also chapter 3.)

The Look Out, Nine Mile Ride, Bracknell RG12 4QW. Telephone: 0344 868222. OS 175: SU 876661. Just south of Bracknell and off B3430 where it links A3095 and A322. The centre has set hours, but the woods are always open.
The Sandhurst ranges are 1 mile (1.6 km) south-southwest of the centre and should be avoided.
This admirable centre was opened in April 1991. There are coffee and gift shops, an audio-visual theatre and special exhibitions. A pleasant and unusual feature is the Look Out Tower, which gives views over the trees.

The centre gives access to 2600 acres (1050 ha) of woodland. Conifers are grown commercially and are mainly Scots pine but there are some Norway spruce. On the edges of the plantations are broad-leaved trees, such as birch and oak. Apart from being attractive in itself, this variety of trees encourages a good variety of plants and wildlife.

From the centre, visitors may follow a forest walk or a nature trail. There is also a heritage trail which leads to some eighteenth-century redoubts and Caesar's Camp (see chapter 3).

Maidenhead Thicket. On the western outskirts of Maidenhead, between A4 towards Reading and A423 towards Henley. There is room to park at the beginning of the track at OS 175: SU 857811, off A423. Open at all times.

Here are over 600 acres (240 ha) of woodland, scrub and grassland. Large numbers of primroses flower in the spring and there are many species of birds, including the nightingale.

Pangbourne Meadow. Beside the Thames at OS 175: SU 640768, 300 yards (270 metres) east of Pangbourne Bridge. Open at all times.

Many interesting plants grow in these 7 acres (2.8 ha) of grassland.

Queen Mother Reservoir, Datchet. The entrance to the reservoir is from Horton Road, between Horton and Colnbrook, at OS 176: TQ 018770.

Public fishing is allowed here, with a permit, which can be obtained from the Queen Mother Fly Fishery, Horton Road, Slough SL3 9NT (telephone: 0753 683605).

The Ridgeway
This, one of the oldest tracks in England, follows the crest of the Berkshire Downs, offering marvellous views, although much of its length was transferred from Berkshire to Oxfordshire in 1974. The easiest place to reach it is where a minor road crosses it, a mile north-northeast of West Ilsley at OS 174: SU 479841. There is plenty of parking space. One of the best views is from Lowbury Hill at SU 540824.

Simon's Wood. North of B3348 between Finchampstead and Crowthorne. There is a car park at OS 175: SU 813635. Open at all times.

The 75 acres (30 ha) contain many species

of trees, including some Scots pines over a hundred years old. A short, pleasant walk leads to Heath Pool.

Here, the B3348 runs along an avenue of wellingtonias, one of the tallest species of tree in the world.

Snelsmore Common. 2½ miles (4 km) north of Newbury, west of B4494, the road to Wantage. There are car parks, which close at dusk, at OS 174: SU 463708. Telephone: Newbury Tourist Information Centre, 0635 30267.

For natural history, this is one of the most important sites in Berkshire. As its 146 acres (59 ha) contain woodland, heathland and bog they attract plants and animals in great variety and abundance. A leaflet on the common is available from Newbury Tourist Information Centre, and there is a full description in Newbury Museum's *Naturalist's Guide to Wild Life around Newbury.*

Near the entrance is a play area with picnic tables.

Sole Common Pond. 4 miles (6 km) west-northwest of Newbury on the north side of B4000 towards Lambourn. There is parking at the beginning of a track at OS 174: SU 414707. Open at all times.

This site is about 2 acres (0.8 ha) of plateau gravels, above chalk. On the north side of the valley is acid heathland, which has been invaded by birch and bracken. On the south side are mature broad-leaved trees. Sphag-

num moss grows in the bottom of the valley. The pond itself is rich in wildlife. Vegetation includes cotton grass, bog-bean and the insectivorous sundew. Birds include wood warblers, woodcocks, siskins and crossbills. Fourteen species of dragonflies have been recorded.

Streatley Hill. West of the village of Streatley. Take B4009 towards Aldworth and Newbury and look for car parks at the top of the hill (OS 174: SU 583806). Open at all times.

A jingle published many years ago in *Punch* runs:

The air is clear, the sky is fine,
The prospect is, I know, divine,
But most distinctly I decline,
To climb the hill at Streatley!

Today, anyone with a vehicle has no need to climb. From the car parks, it is only a gentle stroll north-east across the National Trust properties of Lardon Hill and Lough Down to the brow of the hill, where there is a splendid view of the Goring Gap.

The Thames
Many people have drowned in the Thames. Treat it with respect.

For 50 miles (80 km) the Thames is either flowing through Berkshire or along its northern boundary. Those who wish to explore the riverbanks on foot may be frustrated unless they plan. Access to the river is not allowed at many places and the towpath is incomplete.

The Thames at Streatley.

Boulter's Lock, Maidenhead.

Serious walkers should buy *Rambling for Pleasure along the Thames*, which is mentioned in the introduction to this chapter. For those who just want to take a gentle stroll along the riverbank, some of the best places from which to start are described below.

In 1991 the National Rivers Authority announced that it proposed to make a cut running north of the Thames from Boulter's Lock, Maidenhead, to Black Potts railway bridge, east of Eton. The purpose of the cut is to prevent flooding, but it is sure to attract wildlife.

Anyone who wants to fish must hold a rod and line licence. These licences are on sale at most tackle shops and at most locks. For advice on where fishing is allowed, contact the National Rivers Authority, PO Box 214, Reading RG1 8HQ. Telephone: 0734 535651.

Boulter's Lock, Maidenhead. Beside A4094 towards Cookham, ³/₄ mile (1.2 km) north of its junction with A4 at Maidenhead Bridge (OS 175: SU 903824). There is a car park just north of the lock on the other side of the road.

The 2 miles (3 km) between Boulter's Lock and Cookham are known as Cliveden Reach. It is one of the most beautiful stretches of the Thames and, moreover, it is not without interest. High on the Buckinghamshire side, above its magnificent woods, is Cliveden House. Early in the twentieth century it was bought by an American, William Waldorf Astor, who became head of a group known as the Cliveden Set, notorious for its alleged sympathies with the Nazis. There was notoriety of another kind in the early 1960s. By the water's edge is a cottage that Lord Astor loaned to the osteopath Stephen Ward and where Ward entertained Christine Keeler, so setting in train the events which were to lead to the Profumo scandal of 1963.

Boulter's Weir, Maidenhead.

Hurley. Park near the church at OS 175: SU 824821. East from the lock it is a short, pleasant walk to Temple footbridge. In the opposite direction, the path follows the river for a good 2 miles (3 km). (See also chapters 4 and 9.)

Remenham. Park near the church at OS 175: SU 771842. From here there are good walks in both directions. To the south, it is about a mile (1.6 km) to Henley Bridge. The other way, the path runs for 2 miles (3 km) round a great bend in the river as far as Aston, where there was once a ferry. It soon passes Temple Island, on which stands a delightful folly of 1771, designed by James Wyatt.

Temple Island is the starting point of the Henley Royal Regatta, for which the river has been straightened over the length of the course, 1 mile and 550 yards (2.112 km). The regatta is held each year during the first week of July. At first, all the competitors were 'gentlemen amateurs' and when, just after the First World War, a manual worker called Jack Kelly tried to take part, he was only allowed to do so after a furious row. Anyone can compete now, but the Regatta is still very much a society event.

Pangbourne. Take B471 towards Whitchurch and, while still in Pangbourne, look for a car park on the right immediately after passing under a railway bridge. From here, there is a walk of 2½ miles (4 km) east, to Mapledurham. (See also Pangbourne Meadow, above.)

Thatcham Moor. 2½ miles (4 km) east of Newbury. Take A4 towards Reading and after passing the junction with B4231, fork right along Lower Way Lane. In just over a mile (1.6 km), turn right down the track which comes after the entrance to the sewage farm. There is a car park at OS 174: SU 511666 and a footpath leads south from it over the railway line. The OS map (1989 edition) does not show the full length of the track, the car park or the footpath. Open at all times.

Thatcham Moor is said to be the largest area of inland freshwater reed beds in England. As well as reeds which grow 6 feet (1.8 metres) tall there are numerous species of marshland and aquatic plants such as coltsfoot, butterbur, water crowfoot and sedges. Moths include scarlet tigers, wainscots and china-marks. The moor is especially good for birds.

It is an important breeding ground for reed and sedge warblers; migrating birds like swallows, martins and waders rest here; scarce species have been seen, such as bearded tits, water rails and spotted crakes.

Windsor Great Park. Best approached from the south-east side, where there are car parks. They are marked on OS Landranger map 175. From Windsor take A308 towards Staines and then, after Old Windsor, A328 towards Englefield Green. Look for signs to Savill Garden.

The Park, which is the enormous size of 4800 acres (1940 ha), contains woodland, grassland and water, so there is a good variety of wildlife. The three main lakes are Great Meadow Pond, Obelisk Pond and Virginia Water. Many species of English waterfowl are found on them and there are also mandarin ducks from east Asia. (See also chapter 5.)

Temple Island.

Disc barrow, Lambourn Seven Barrows.

3
Places of archaeological interest

Caesar's Camp, Bracknell (OS 175: SU 864655). Parking at The Look Out (SU 876661).

This iron age fort encloses 20 acres (8 ha). There is an impressive bank and ditch with a counterscarp in places. The north entrance is approached between two long parallel banks. The fort is covered with trees, making it a pleasant place to walk. Just under a mile south-southeast are some eighteenth-century redoubts. They were built to train militia during the Napoleonic Wars. (See also The Look Out, chapter 2.)

Calleva Roman town. Just east of Silchester, Hampshire (OS 175: SU 643623). The signposts say 'Roman Wall'.

Calleva Museum, which is also signposted, should be visited before the town (chapter 6). Most of the finds from early excavations are in Reading Museum (chapter 6), but those from the excavations in the 1980s are in the care of the Hampshire Museums Service.

Calleva was the capital of the Atrebates, one of the more advanced tribes of Roman Britain. The town was excavated thoroughly in Victorian and Edwardian times, but everything that was uncovered has since been buried to protect it. None the less, this is still the most impressive Roman town in Britain because the site has hardly any later buildings on it and because the circuit of the walls is complete. These walls are 1½ miles (2.4 km) long and enclose an area of 107 acres (43 ha). In places they still stand 15 feet (4.5 metres)

high, the best preserved parts being between the church and the south gate. The walls are built mainly of flint, though from time to time the builders put in courses of flat slabs of limestone to keep their work level and vertical. The mortar is as hard as iron, which is more than modern concrete will be 1700 years from now.

To the north-east of the town is the amphitheatre. Gladiators may have fought at *Calleva*, but it is unlikely, since they were expensive for a provincial town to hire. Any blood that flowed would have come from animals, criminals or, possibly, Christians, while most of the shows would have been athletics.

Grim's Bank, near Padworth. This can be walked from the corner of the wood at OS 175: SU 623658. It is more impressive at the road junction at SU 612640, though here it is on private land.

The origins of Grim's Bank are obscure, but it seems that it was built by the inhabitants of *Calleva*, as a defence against the Saxons, who were advancing up the Thames.

'Grim' is a nickname for Woden, and he, in Christian times, was seen as a devil. People often ascribed such massive works as Grim's Bank to supernatural powers.

Grimsbury Castle, Hermitage (OS 174: SU 512723). Just to the south-east of Hermitage, off the minor road to Bucklebury. A road leads through the camp, so there is no climb.

This is a small iron age fort enclosing 8 acres (3.2 ha). It is covered with trees, but there is little dense undergrowth. In the centre is a delightful octagonal tower, perhaps built as a folly, but now used as a house.

For the name, see under Grim's Bank.

Grim's Ditch. There are lengths of Grim's Ditch in a number of places, but an especially good section runs from the track at OS 174: SU 467851, on East Hendred Down. From here it goes east along the face of the chalk escarpment to the A34.

It seems that much of Grim's Ditch dates from the iron age though parts of it are probably later. It could well have been used to check the Saxons.

For the name, see under Grim's Bank. According to legend, the Devil ploughed Grim's Ditch in a single night, two round barrows near Streatley being the scrapings from his ploughshare.

Inkpen Beacon, Combe Gibbet, Combe (OS 174: SU 364623).

This neolithic long barrow on Inkpen Beacon is close to the car park and viewpoint that lie at the top of the hill on the minor road between Inkpen and Combe. The barrow is impressive, being 164 feet (50 metres) long, 49 feet (15 metres) wide and 6½ feet (2 metres) high, with side ditches 3¼ feet (1 metre) deep. (See also chapter 2.)

Lambourn Seven Barrows, Lambourn (OS 174: SU 329828).

This is one of the most impressive bronze age barrow cemeteries in England. In spite of the name, there are at least 32 barrows but the best group is north-west of a small car park a few yards along a track off the Lambourn to Kingston Lisle road, at the map reference given above.

This group contains six bowl barrows, two double bowl barrows, two saucer barrows and one disc barrow. A bowl barrow is like a bowl turned upside down whilst a saucer barrow has a much smaller mound. A disc barrow has a small central mound surrounded, at a few yards from it, by a low, circular bank and ditch. Usually, each bronze age barrow was for just one individual, disc barrows being for women and bowl barrows for people of either sex.

The barrows were constructed of chalk and when they were first made their surfaces were bare, making them stand out, startlingly white, against the landscape. (See also chapter 2.)

Robin Hood's Arbour, Maidenhead Thicket (OS 175: SU 853811). Park where track joins A423 at SU 857811.

This farm enclosure of about ¾ acre (0.3 ha), which was in use just before the Roman conquest, is surrounded by a low bank and a shallow ditch. Some sherds of Celtic pottery were found in it and a sunken paved area which may have been a stockyard. (See also chapter 2 for Maidenhead Thicket.)

Walbury Hill, between Inkpen and Combe (OS 174: SU 374617).

This is an iron age hillfort defended only by a slight bank and ditch, but its size is impressive, for it covers 82 acres (33 ha). It stands on Berkshire's highest hill and commands wonderful views. (See also chapter 2.)

The walls of Calleva.

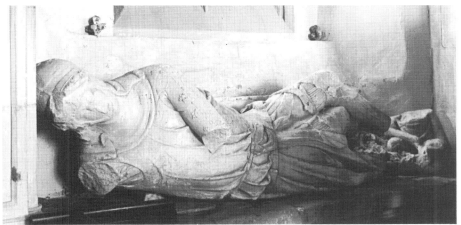

Aldworth, St Mary: tomb of Sir Philip de la Beche.

4
Churches

Berkshire has no cathedral and because of the lack of good building stone its parish churches cannot, in general, compare with those of such areas as Somerset or the Cotswolds. Moreover, the humble nature of many delightful Berkshire churches proved their undoing, for the Tractarian clergy of the nineteenth century considered such buildings unworthy and either ruined them with ambitious alterations or replaced them entirely.

There are, though, compensations. In the late fifteenth and early sixteenth centuries, when English church architecture was at its peak, four magnificent royal chapels were built. They are Henry VII's chantry at Westminster Abbey and the chapels of King's College, Cambridge, Eton College and Windsor Castle. Of these four, two are in Berkshire. They are described in chapter 8.

One decided advantage which Berkshire has over most counties is its nineteenth- and early twentieth-century stained glass. Easthampstead and Cranbourne churches are art galleries of the works of William Morris, Edward Burne-Jones and others of their generation, while there are some superb windows by Frank Brangwyn at Bucklebury. Laurence Whistler designed the beautiful engraved glass windows at Eastbury in commemoration of the poet Edward Thomas and his wife, Helen.

Three churches are outstanding: Newbury, Lambourn and Shottesbrooke. Two churches, Avington and Padworth, are almost pure Norman, and so is Enborne, apart from its chancel. For the rest, the typical Berkshire church is built in a medley of styles and is quite modest, with a squat Perpendicular tower or a timber bellcote. Nearly all of them, though, are a pleasure to visit and many contain delightful surprises, such as the giants at Aldworth, the swans at Bisham, the elephants at Wickham and the fly on the window at Bucklebury.

Aldworth: St Mary.

The main attraction here is eight early fourteenth-century tombs, each bearing an effigy. They belonged to the de la Beche family, who owned a castle locally. The most remarkable effigy is the one said to be of Sir Philip de la Beche; he is lying on his side, raised on his elbow and, apparently, writhing in discomfort. Sir Philip joined an unsuccessful rebellion against Richard II, was imprisoned for five years and had his lands confiscated.

The villagers called the effigies the 'Aldworth Giants' and gave them names like John Long, John Strong, and John Never Afraid. Legend says there was also a John Ever Afraid. His soul was to go to the Devil if he was buried in a church or churchyard, so

17

he was put in an arch under the church wall. This tomb, if it ever existed, has vanished.

The effigies are somewhat defaced, but they are still impressive and when they were new and, presumably, painted and gilded, they must have been magnificent.

The canopies over the tombs were restored with an excess of enthusiasm in the 1870s.

Above the columns in the aisle are grotesque carvings of dogs' heads. The pulpit and the reader's desk could be the work of a craftsman from the Low Countries.

In the churchyard are the sad remains of a yew tree which is said to be a thousand years old.

Ashampstead: St Clement.

The church has a thirteenth-century nave and chancel, with several of the original slender lancet windows which were typical of the period. Built into the north-west corner is the stump of a yew, preserved, according to legend, because services were held under the tree before the church was built. The timber bell-turret with its shingle-covered spire is characteristic of Berkshire.

What makes this church truly remarkable is its thirteenth-century wall paintings. The most impressive of these is a group on the north wall of the nave, depicting an Annunciation, a

Avington, St Mark and St Luke: Norman doorway.

Avington, St Mark and St Luke: Norman font.

Visitation, a Nativity and an Appearance of the Angel to the Shepherds. Other paintings include a St Christopher, who is just opposite the door so that any traveller could have a quick blessing and continue his journey without delay.

Avington: St Mark and St Luke.

The church lies in a secluded spot, surrounded by trees. It is almost pure Norman.

The building is only a simple rectangle in plan, but there is a wealth of carving. The south doorway is covered with zigzag, while the chancel arch has another typical Norman ornament, beakheads. These have large eyes and long, pointed noses which wrap around the moulding. On each side of the chancel is a pilaster, so either there was a stone vault at some time, or one was planned.

The chief delight is the Norman font. It is carved with eleven arches containing figures. They include a bishop, a man with raised hands, a devil, a pair kissing and another pair who might be Satan tempting Judas.

Bisham: All Saints.

The church is in a splendid position, right by the Thames and with moorings for boats. There is an attractive Norman west tower, but the Victorians restored the body of the church so thoroughly as to spoil it. The main attraction here is the three Hoby tombs in the south chapel. They are of the late sixteenth and early seventeenth centuries. All were commissioned by Elizabeth, Lady Hoby.

The earliest of the tombs carries the alabaster effigies of two knights representing Elizabeth's first husband, Sir Thomas Hoby, and his half-brother, Sir Philip.

Next is Elizabeth's own tomb. It is dominated by the lady herself, clad in sumptuous widow's weeds and attended by her children. A daughter kneels in front of her, while three daughters and two sons kneel behind her. Immediately in front of her is the recumbent forlorn figure of her little boy and there is a story that she beat him to death for smudging his copy book. It is said that her ghost haunts Bisham Priory, lamenting her crime. A copy book was found at the priory, written in Elizabethan handwriting and with marks that might well have been caused by tears.

The third tomb, that of Elizabeth's daughter-in-law Margaret, is entirely original and quite delightful. It has a high plinth on which stands an obelisk ending in a heart. Also on the plinth, at its corners, are four swans with their wings spread.

In the chancel there is a tomb-chest of Purbeck marble, with a pretty canopy and vault. It is like one at Cookham.

Bucklebury: St Mary.

The church was originally Norman, but there is little evidence of that now, save the splendid south doorway. As well as the characteristic zigzag ornament there are flowers, rosettes and several faces, including a fierce one at the top, surmounted by an orb and a cross. The tower is Perpendicular. On its south face is a carving of a man with a wheel, or winch. The manor had belonged to Reading Abbey, but at the Dissolution in 1540 Henry VIII sold it to John Winchcombe, son of the famous Jack of Newbury (chapter 9). The carving is said to be the Winchcombe rebus.

Bisham, All Saints: tomb of Elizabeth, Lady Hoby.

Bisham, All Saints: tomb of Margaret Hoby.

The north arcade was cut in the original Norman walls when the aisle was added in the thirteenth century. The church has kept its eighteenth-century box pews. Among the furniture is a magnificent oak chest which may have come from Reading Abbey. It has nine locks, all of which work together at one turn of the key. Over the squire's pew is a stained glass window showing a sundial and, beside it, a fly. The fly looks realistic because its body is on one side of the glass and its wings on the other. Most remarkable, however, are the stained glass windows of 1912, by Frank Brangwyn. The colours glow richly, without being gaudy, while the scenes are both dramatic and realistic. Some of the faces could have been painted by Breughel.

In the late seventeenth century the manor passed to Frances Winchcombe, who married Henry St John, Viscount Bolingbroke. He was Secretary of State to Queen Anne. For a time Bucklebury attracted many distinguished guests. Alexander Pope worshipped in the church and Dean Swift may have preached here. In 1714, after he had run through his wife's fortune and lost his position as Secretary of State, Bolingbroke fled to France, where he found another woman. Lady Bolingbroke died, aged 39, broken-hearted and in debt.

Left: *Bucklebury, St Mary: window by Frank Brangwyn.*

20

Bucklebury, St Mary: Norman doorway.

Cranbourne: St Peter.

This Victorian church has some superb stained glass. The west window is by William Morris, who designed Cana, Ford Madox Brown, who designed Christ and a child, and Philip Webb, who designed the ornament. In the south wall, just west of the door, is a striking two-light window depicting St Peter and Cornelius. It was designed by Selwyn Image.

The south chapel is dedicated in honour of Field Marshal the Earl Alexander of Tunis.

Douai Abbey Church: St Edmund. This is near Woolhampton at OS 174: SU 577683.

In 1903 the French government expelled the Benedictines and those from Douai built themselves a monastery and a boys' school here. The abbey church was begun in 1928 to the designs of J. Arnold Crush. The chancel was completed, along with two bays of the nave, but then work stopped, a temporary wall being built to close the open end of the nave. There are plans to finish the church in 1992.

Right: *Cranborne, St Peter: window by Selwyn Image.*

 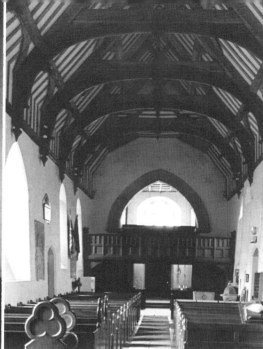

Left: *Douai Abbey.*

Right: *Hampstead Norreys, St Mary.*

The outside of the building is red brick, relieved only by a couple of bands of flint panels in stone surrounds. The interior, in marked contrast, is of ashlar, and is brilliantly white. As it is vaulted throughout, there are not even any roof timbers to darken it.

The style is in imitation of Decorated, the most flamboyant of the middle ages, and, whereas a nineteenth-century architect would have crammed in many of its motifs, Crush used hardly any ornament at all. The windows do have some stained glass, but it is so subtle that the colours are hardly noticeable. The combined result is that, though the church may be severe, it is light, spacious and beautiful.

Easthampstead: St Michael and St Mary Magdalene.

Here there is Victorian stained glass of the highest quality, including five windows designed by Edward Burne-Jones and made by William Morris. They are as follows:
North aisle, north wall, westmost: left, angel with palm and lyre; centre, St Michael; right, angel with palm and violin.

North aisle, north wall, eastmost: the story of St Maurice. He was a Roman general who was martyred for refusing to sacrifice to Mars after a victory.
North aisle, east wall: left, St Mary Magdalene at the empty sepulchre; right, Christ and St Mary Magdalene in the garden.
Chancel, north wall, eastmost: Adoration of the Magi.
Chancel, east window: the Last Judgement.

The east window of the chancel is the climax. It is of three large lights, with a rose above. The rose depicts Christ sitting in judgement, surrounded by six angels in small circles. Below is St Michael in armour. Behind him, the Blessed sit in rows, there are angels on either side and, in front, the dead rise from their graves.

There are copies of the rose in at least eight English churches and in Newcastle Cathedral, New South Wales.

Enborne: St Michael and All Angels.

Apart from its Victorian south side, this is a delightful church. The original building was

22

Saxon or early Norman and was just a nave and a chancel. Aisles were added in about 1150 and the church was extended westwards by one bay. As all this work was done in a single campaign, the sturdy Norman columns are fairly uniform, giving the building a pleasing unity.

The chancel was enlarged in the thirteenth century. Beside the altar is a splendid fourteenth-century painting that might be an Annunciation or Christ at the well with the woman of Samaria.

The church has a bell cast in 1220 which must be among the oldest in England.

Eton: College Chapel (see chapter 8).

Great Fawley: St Mary the Virgin.
This church was built by G. E. Street in the 1860s. In contrast with most Victorian churches, St Mary's has but little ornament and though the result is severe it is pleasing. Street used Early English motifs. For example, the chancel has simple quadripartite vaulting, there is a good deal of marble and there is a line of nailhead round the chancel arch. However, this is not a slavish copy of an Early English church. It has an apse, where a square-ended chancel would be more correct; the tower is in the wrong place and the short sturdy drum columns look Norman. These and many other such features are not mistakes but a deliberate attempt to create something original. It has been most successful.

The first, general impression of St Mary's is, however, more striking than any of the detail. The nave, though splendid, is quite gloomy, so on entering it the eyes are drawn immediately where they should go, to the chancel. This is raised high above the nave, its white walls and vaulting bathed in light.

Great Shefford: St Mary.
There is a splendid approach to the church, along an avenue of limes and through a stone arch. After that, the church itself is a disappointment, apart from the tower, which is the only original round one in Berkshire. Probably it is Norman.

Hampstead Norreys: St Mary.
Parts of the building are, perhaps, much older than appears. For example, the quoins in the south-west corner of the nave might be Saxon. The chancel is Early English, that is early thirteenth-century, with the slender lancet windows of the period. The north and south doorways are the same style. The nave has a fine roof, with pendants, which was built in 1635.

Opposite the north door is a thirteenth-century painting of the Virgin, much faded. In a glass case, also opposite the door, is a striking little sculpture of a knight, charging on a prancing horse. Why the stone was carved is not known but for a long time it was misused as a step to one of the church doorways.

South of the church is a cast iron monument of about 1850, to the Lowsley family. Some say that their labourers searched local farmyards for scrap iron to make the monument. It is in poor condition.

Hurley: St Mary.
St Mary's is an odd shape, being long, narrow and tall. The probable reason is that it was the nave of a Saxon priory church, for these proportions are typically Saxon. The chancel of the original church has gone.

Beside the altar is an Elizabethan monument, with two kneeling figures, of Richard Lovelace and his son John. High on the east wall is a wooden cross. It is said to date from 1040, which would make it the oldest wooden cross in England. (See also chapter 2, under Thames, and chapter 9.)

Lambourn: St Michael and All Angels.
St Michael's is one of the finest parish churches in Berkshire.

The original church was Norman, on the cruciform plan. It had a nave, aisles, a central tower, transepts and a chancel which, if it was true to its period, would have been an apse. The transepts were rebuilt, the north one in the thirteenth century and its fellow in the early fourteenth century. Even more work was done during the late fourteenth and fifteenth centuries, in the Perpendicular style. The tower was made taller, the new storey having fine belfry openings, battlements and pinnacles. At the east end a large chancel was built, flanked by chapels, one on the north and two on the south. The outer south chapel is quite ornate, with battlements and pinnacles to match those on the tower.

The west end still has the original Norman doorway, with its zigzag ornament. There is a circular Norman window in the gable and Norman windows to the aisles. The large window above the door was added in the early fourteenth century, so it is in the Decorated style, with flowing tracery.

The nave arcades are Norman, with solid round pillars and semicircular arches. The arches of the crossing tower are Norman, too, but they are pointed, showing that they belong to the end of their period. The arch at the east end of the north aisle is interrupted by a flying buttress, which was put in for extra support when the tower was heightened. Another curiosity is the piscina on the east wall of the nave, about 13 feet (4 metres) from the ground. It shows there must have been a rood loft here at one time.

On the wall of the south aisle, near the arch leading to the Lady Chapel, is an alabaster medallion of Charles I, with the figures of Truth and Justice standing on Puritans in chains. The medallion was put here in 1893 and may have come from Lambourn Place.

The chancel, with its splendid five-light window, is Perpendicular. On the north wall of the sanctuary is the Elizabethan tomb of Thomas and Agnes Garrard. It has two kneeling figures and a sad inscription. On the south wall of the chancel is a brass to two more Garrards, another Thomas and his wife, Alice. This brass gives an excellent idea of early Jacobean costume.

St Katherine's Chapel, north of the chancel, contains the alabaster tomb of Sir Thomas Essex of Lambourn Place and his wife, Margaret. Sir Thomas died in 1558, the year Elizabeth I came to the throne. At this time it was common for tombs to show a great many Renaissance features, but all this one has to offer is some rudimentary balusters.

South of the chancel is St Mary's Chapel. The main interest here is the carving on the west side of the archway into the transept. The two corbels are grotesque, one being the head of a woman wearing a wimple, and the other a man with buttons along his sleeves. In the hollows of the jambs there are faces, including a bishop and a jester. Most beguiling of all is a hunting scene carved in tiny figures round the arch. There are also trout, for which Lambourn was once famous, though none come so far up the river today. Often, there is not even any water.

Beside St Mary's Chapel is Holy Trinity Chapel, which contains the tomb of John of Estbury. It was he who, in 1501, founded the almshouses to the north of the church. They were for ten old men, who came daily to pray round the tomb of their benefactor. They no longer do so, though the cold hard seats are still in place. According to legend, the unfortunate John died when a worm fell into his mouth while he was sleeping in his garden.

Outside, it is worth finding the tomb of John Carter, who met his end in an equally unpleasant but more common way. The tomb is to the north of the church, near the railings and opposite the almshouses.

Langley Marish: St Mary.

St Mary's has a little Norman work in its west front, but most of the body of the church is Decorated, that is early fourteenth-century. The tower and the Kederminster Chapel are brick and of the early seventeenth century.

Inside there are two galleries, one strangely placed on the south side of the tower, and one in the north aisle.

The screen to the Kederminster Chapel is of Coade stone, an artificial stone invented in the late eighteenth century by Eleanor Coade, born in Lyme Regis. It carves well and is very durable. In the chancel is a monument of 1599, to the Kederminster family. An almost pagan touch is three carvings of the mythical 'green men'. They are in the chancel, on the corbels, the stones from which the arches spring. The font is Perpendicular, probably fifteenth-century.

St Mary's is an interesting and attractive church in its own right, but the main reason for braving the Slough traffic to come here is to see the Kederminster Library. This, a collection of three hundred religious books, was presented to the church by the lord of the manor, Sir John Kederminster, early in the seventeenth century. Since then no books have been added and, indeed, the library is still exactly as it was when it was founded. This must surely make it unique. To see the library, it is necessary to make an appointment with the curator, currently Mrs Muriel Kemp of 15 Springate Field, Langley Marish.

Flanking the churchyard are two terraces of almshouses. The one to the south was, like the library, the gift of Sir John Kederminster.

Newbury: St Nicolas.

There was once a Norman church on this site, but it was replaced by a new one built entirely between 1500 and 1532. As a result, the present church belongs to the late Perpendicular period, a golden age for ecclesiastical architecture. Also no expense was spared, since John Smallwood (Jack of Newbury),

Newbury, St Nicolas: the pulpit of 1607.

blems, the series ends with the sword of St Peter and the head of Judas with a rope round it. There are numerous bosses in the roof, all beautifully carved. Some bear John Smallwood's monogram, an I and an S intertwined.

The magnificent pulpit dates from 1607. It has two tiers of deep-set panels, the top row in square frames and the lower row in arches.

By the north door is a cut-out of a Blue Coat boy. In the eighteenth century it was the fashion to found charity schools. They were for a select few children of the 'deserving poor' who were taught the religion of the Church of England and were trained to become docile servants and apprentices. Such schools were usually named after the colour of their uniform, which was provided free. Newbury founded its charity school in 1706. The present cut-out is a copy of the original, which stood over an almsbox intended for donations to the school.

The chapels beside the chancel were built as chantries, places where masses were said for the souls of the dead. This practice ended in the reign of Edward VI, and the south chapel at Newbury became, for a time, a boys' school. It is now the Lady Chapel, while its fellow is the vestry.

The sixteenth-century building did not escape unscathed. Betjeman remarks laconically: 'The church was restored in 1867 by H. Woodyer and far too frequently after that.' Also the windows are filled with mediocre Victorian stained glass, making the interior dark.

Fuller White built the east gateways to the churchyard in 1770. They are Gothic Revival and the earliest examples of this style in Berkshire.

Padworth: St John the Baptist.

The church is tucked away at the end of a rough track. There is a magnificent yew in the graveyard.

Apart from some Perpendicular windows and a Victorian porch and vestry, St John's is entirely Norman. It has the simplest of Norman plans, just a nave and an apse, and it is interesting to find the latter still intact. Many a priest decided that his small semicircular apse cramped his style and had it replaced by a larger square-ended chancel. The chancel arch is unusually large and magnificent for a church of this size.

Captain Clinton's monument has an interesting inscription.

the wealthy merchant who paid for the nave, was determined to make a splendid gift to the town.

The church has a nave, aisles, a west tower and a chancel flanked by two chapels. It is in ashlar, the most expensive form of building stone. The walls are pierced by large windows and capped by battlements. The 70 foot (21 metre) tower is especially striking, with its polygonal buttresses ending in large pinnacles. Formerly pancakes were thrown from the tower on Shrove Tuesday and children scrambled for them. Until the advent of greaseproof paper, these pancakes were unwrapped.

The nave is of five bays, the arcades having the characteristic four-centred arches of the Perpendicular style. The nave has kept its original roof. Among the corbels are angels with shields bearing the emblems of the Passion, such as the dice which the soldiers threw when casting lots for Christ's garments. As there were more angels than there are em-

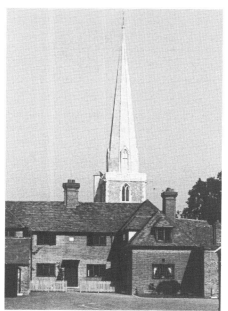

Shottesbrooke church spire.

Tidmarsh, St Laurence: Norman doorway.

Shottesbrooke: St John the Baptist. (Between White Waltham and Waltham St Lawrence.)

The church stands in an attractive park, well away from ordinary houses, and it may be that the lord of the manor destroyed the village of Shottesbrooke when he laid out this park in the seventeenth century.

Sir William Trussell founded the church in 1337. According to legend, he did so as an act of thanksgiving, for he drank himself nearly to death but recovered unexpectedly. Trussell also founded a college of a warden, five priests and two clerks. The college has long gone, but the church remains, and it is one of the finest of its period in England.

The building is cruciform in plan, that is, with a nave, chancel, north and south transepts and a crossing tower, capped with a magnificent spire. The chancel is longer than the nave because the college of priests needed plenty of room to officiate. The style is Decorated, as is shown by the flowing lines of the window tracery. A favourite Decorated motif, found in many parts of the church, is the ogee curve. It follows, roughly, the outline of the onion-shaped domes of Greek Orthodox churches.

In the fourteenth century the windows were painted with numerous heraldic shields and the church was 'ablaze with heraldry'. Unfortunately only six of these shields remain, but there is a good deal of clear glass, so that the interior is light.

The founder and his wife are buried in the north transept. Their tombs have elaborate canopies with ogee arches. An interesting tomb belongs to a priest, William Throckmorton, who died in 1535. His effigy is interrupted by a stone lying across his waist and bearing a brass, with inscriptions. Near the founder's tomb is a brass to one Noke, 'who for his great age and vertuous lief was reverenced of all men and comenly called Father Noke, created Esquier by Henry VIII. He had in his lief three Wifes, and by every of them some Fruyte and ofsprynge.' Among other brasses there is a particularly fine one of a priest and a layman.

From the churchyard it is possible to see Shottesbrooke Park, with its castellated parapet. This is a house of the sixteenth and seventeenth centuries which was 'gothicised' in about 1810. 41 of its rooms were demolished in the early twentieth century.

In the late seventeenth century this was the

Theale, Holy Trinity.

home of Francis Cherry, who turned it into a refuge for non-jurors, that is, people who refused to take the oath of allegiance to William III. Once, Cherry was in a hunting party which included the King. Noticing that William was sticking closely to him, he made a dangerous jump over a bank of the Thames in the hope that the monarch would follow him and break his neck. The trick failed.

Theale: Holy Trinity.

This striking church was built between 1820 and 1832. The style is Early English, some of the motifs being copied from Salisbury Cathedral, notably the buttresses at the west end. The architect did not scale down these motifs to suit a parish church, but this was deliberate. Using old ideas in new ways was one of the tricks that nineteenth-century builders used to create something original. The plan of the church is original, too. There is a projecting west porch, which no thirteenth-century cathedral would have, and the tower is oddly placed. It is apart from the main building but connected to it by an open passage at ground level and, above it, by a wing containing a library.

Tidmarsh: St Laurence.

Three things make this church remarkable. In the first place, it has the finest Norman doorway in Berkshire. It is richly carved, not only with the usual zigzag, but with many other ornaments as well. Above it is a stern, scowling face. Secondly, the bell-turret is supported by massive, scissor-braced timbers which stand inside the church. Early in the twentieth century the then vicar's wife carved them with decoration copied from the doorway. Thirdly, the church has a thirteenth-century Early English polygonal apse, which is most unusual for the period. The apse is found in all styles on the continent, but in England it is a Romanesque feature, confined almost always to Saxon and Norman churches.

Warfield: St Michael the Archangel.

Much of the stone in this church is brown conglomerate so that from the outside the building looks somewhat gloomy and austere. This is misleading, for St Michael's is one of the most enjoyable churches in Berkshire.

The north aisle, which was the original

church, was built in the thirteenth century so it is in the Early English style, with one narrow lancet window and traces of others. The rest of the body of the building is early fourteenth-century and in the Decorated style. Several of the windows have fairly simple intersecting tracery, but the east window of the chancel has a complicated pattern of flowing lines. The tower is Perpendicular, probably fifteenth-century.

The north chapel has a rood screen, which is unusual in Berkshire, while above it is a rood loft, which would be unusual anywhere in England.

The roofs to the north aisle and the nave are fine examples of medieval carpentry.

The chancel is the most interesting and attractive part of the church. A curious feature here is the low screen behind the altar, enclosing a narrow space between it and the east wall. This space may have been a relic chamber. The screen is Victorian, but it is an authentic copy of the one it replaced. On the south wall are sedilia and a piscina made from hard chalk, beautifully and elaborately carved. There are ogee arches, gables with crockets and finials and much foliage.

On the south wall of the chancel is a monument to Thomas Williamson, who died in 1611. He had, it would seem, eight sons and eight daughters. There are two more monuments of much the same date on the east wall of the north chapel. Also in the chapel are the sad remains of three canopied tomb recesses which must once have been like those at Aldworth.

South of the church are the Parish Room and St Michael's Grange, both of the seventeenth century.

Sir William Herschel, who developed the system of identification by fingerprints, once lived at Warfield Rectory.

Wasing: St Nicholas.

The church is in the middle of a park, but visitors may drive to it through any of the lodge gates.

St Nicholas's began as a small medieval

Left: *Waltham St Lawrence. See chapter 9.*

Right: *Wickham, St Swithun: Saxon tower. The top storey is Victorian.*

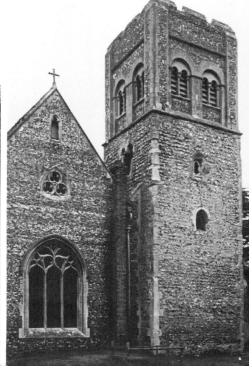

church with just a chancel and a short nave. In the eighteenth century the south transept was added and the nave extended, so giving the church its Georgian look. Formerly the bell-turret was at the west end and it is because of the extension that it is now in its curious position, halfway along the nave.

There is some old stained glass in the nave, one piece bearing the date 1649. The main attraction of the interior, though, is the plasterwork around the windows. It looks Victorian but is said to be eighteenth-century.

Wasing Place, next to the church, was built in the 1770s, burnt down during the Second World War and rebuilt, as far as possible, with the old materials.

Wickham: St Swithun.

Benjamin Ferrey completely rebuilt the body of this church in the 1840s. He copied the Decorated style and the result is highly ornate. The walls are for the most part of knapped, or squared, flints, though there are places which show that the masons sometimes tired of the very tedious task of shaping them.

The two attractions here are the elephants and the Saxon tower. The elephants, of papier-mâché, appear to support the aisle roof. They were bought at the Paris Exhibition of 1862 and intended for the rectory, but as they proved too large for it they were put in the church.

The top storey of the tower is Victorian, but the rest is Anglo-Saxon, making it unique in Berkshire. The quoins show the characteristic 'long and short' work. Some of the smaller windows have semicircular heads and are splayed outside. The larger windows are of twin lights, separated by a baluster shaft. Anglo-Saxon masons did not know how to cut arch stones and those in the south twin-light window are irregular. The ones in the north window, though, are correctly made, showing that they are replacements.

Windsor: St George's Chapel (see chapter 8).

Winkfield: St Mary.

Here, there is an early seventeenth-century tower, which is entirely of brick, even the window tracery. The plan of the church is unusual in that there are two naves, but what is truly remarkable, though not beautiful, is the wooden arcade separating them. It was made in 1592. The columns are said to be cut from whole tree trunks of Windsor Forest oaks.

When G. E. Street rebuilt the chancel in 1858 he made it tripartite, so that its centre is in line with the arcade, an awkward arrangement.

Above the pulpit is a brass to Thomas Montague, a Yeoman of the Guard who died in 1630, aged 92. He is shown giving alms.

Basildon Park.

5
Historic buildings and gardens

Basildon Park, Lower Basildon, Reading RG8 9NR. Telephone: 0734 843040. National Trust.

Basildon Park is Berkshire's premier mansion. It was built between 1776 and 1783 by Francis Sykes, an official of the East India Company. He came home with a large fortune, much of it embezzled from the revenues of Bengal. As he put it, 'It was this, whether it would go into a black man's pocket or my own.'

The architect employed by Sykes was the brilliant John Carr of York. The house itself was completed at the time, but, oddly, Sykes did not finish the interiors of some of the most important rooms.

Sykes's son and grandson were spendthrifts, so in 1838 the house was sold to James Morrison, a London haberdasher. He may or may not have coined the motto 'small profits, quick returns', but he certainly lived by it. He also had a good eye for an opportunity. When Queen Caroline died in 1821 and the rest of the nation was stricken with grief, Morrison cornered the market in black crêpe. He made an art collection and, needing a 'casket to enclose pictorial gems', he bought Basildon.

Morrison employed J. B. Papworth to finish the interiors which Francis Sykes had left incomplete.

The Morrison family abandoned Basildon Park in 1910, and in 1928 Lord Iliffe, the owner of the *Daily Mail*, bought it. Almost at once he resold to one George Ferdinando, who made plans to transport it stone by stone to the United States. Fortunately, he was able to move only enough to decorate the Basildon Room of the Waldorf Astoria Hotel.

The nadir of Basildon's fortunes came during the Second World War when tanks exercised in the park and soldiers billeted in the house scrawled on the walls and smashed windows. The place was saved when, in 1952, Lord Iliffe's son bought and restored it.

Basildon Park is in the Palladian style, which follows the principles of Roman architecture accurately. It is built of that finest of materials, Bath stone. The façade has seven elements, the dominant one being the central block. Its ground floor is rusticated, which means that the joints in the stonework are made to look thick and this has the effect of seeming to anchor the building firmly to the ground. Above is a loggia running the height of two storeys and fronted with four Ionic pillars. Either side of the main block are two pavilions, each of two storeys and capped with pediments. They were for the services, like the kitchen and the laundry. Linking the pavilions and the main block and forming the ends of the façade are what seem to be four single-storey blocks. They are, though, the front walls of courtyards which contained such things as privies and coal sheds. Holding all seven elements together are two unbroken lines, which take the form of mouldings in some places and the tops and bottoms of balustrades in others.

A peculiarity of Basildon Park is the entrance. Like most great houses of the period, the main rooms are on the first floor, the *piano nobile*. Normally this is reached by as grand a staircase as the owner could afford, but at Basildon one goes first into a somewhat poky lower loggia and then climbs narrow, twisting stairs to the main loggia. Possibly the idea behind this humble approach was to create a contrast with the splendours which greet one on arrival, making them seem even more magnificent.

Fourteen marvellous rooms are open to the public. The Upper Entrance Hall, the Staircase Hall and the Octagon are particularly good. The Upper Entrance Hall and the Green Drawing Room have ceilings with the light delicate patterns of the Robert Adam style.

The word 'Basildon' is well known because the head of the papermaking firm of Dickinson once visited the house and decided to use its name for a notepaper.

Bearwood College, Wokingham RG11 5BG. Telephone: 0734 781729. *This is a working school and visitors are admitted only by appointment.*

Bearwood College traces its traditions back to 1827. Previously known as the Royal Merchant Navy School, it was originally founded to provide a boarding-school education for the orphaned children of merchant seamen. The school now offers a broad-based curriculum on a fee-paying basis but retains close links with the Royal Merchant Navy School Foundation, which continues to support children at Bearwood and other independent schools.

The house is one of the great Victorian buildings of England. Robert Kerr designed it for the owner of *The Times*, John Walter III, and it was finished in about 1870. The style is perhaps best described as Jacobean, freely interpreted, with French Renaissance features.

Bearwood College: north front.

The right-hand section of the north front is a unit. In the centre is a deep porte-cochère and above it is a tower which is reminiscent of French *châteaux* and Belgian town halls. Either side of the tower is a straight-sided gable. Any symmetry there might have been, though, is ruthlessly destroyed by the huge staircase tower superimposed on the left-hand gable. Further left, everything is quite irregular. A great wing juts forward and in the angle is a smaller staircase tower which is quite French in its design.

Two-thirds of the south front are taken up by a unit which is symmetrical with but few interruptions, though the remainder is irregular. At the end is a square tower with an openwork parapet. Great bay windows look over the grounds while the skyline is picturesque with chimney stacks, Flemish gables and domes of assorted shapes and sizes.

The porte-cochère leads to the screens passage of the entrance hall which has been described, unkindly, as 'ham Jacobean'. Beyond the hall is the ground floor of the main staircase tower, while the screens passage opens into the picture gallery.

The approach to the college is along a fine avenue of wellingtonias while the grounds contain cedars, junipers, rhododendrons and many other trees and shrubs. There is also a

40 acre (16 ha) lake. John Walter's son was drowned in it, the very year that the house was finished.

Donnington Castle, just north of Newbury. English Heritage. The site is unattended and open during the day.

With the important exception of Windsor, Donnington is the only medieval castle of any consequence in Berkshire. It was built in the early fourteenth century. In 1386 a licence to strengthen it was granted and the existing gatehouse was put up. During the Civil War Sir John Boys held it for the King, taking over command two days after the first battle of Newbury in 1643. He defended it most valiantly during the siege that lasted from 31st July 1644 to 1st April 1646, keeping possession of it until Charles I himself surrendered.

The curtain wall and towers of the castle have been levelled almost to their foundations, but the gatehouse is intact. The angular earth ramparts around it are the remains of artillery bastions, built during the Civil War.

In Donnington village, on the west side of the B4494 towards Newbury, are some almshouses which were founded in 1393, though the present buildings are seventeenth-century. They are in red brick, one-storeyed and built round a courtyard. The arms on the

Dorney Court.

Donnington Castle.

front are those of Elizabeth I, who restored the revenues of the almshouses which had been confiscated by her father, Henry VIII.

Dorney Court, Dorney, Windsor SL4 6QP. Telephone: 0628 604638.

Dorney Court is a manor house. Its oldest parts date from the fifteenth century, which was before the Renaissance imposed its many rules, including that of symmetry, on English builders. As a result the outside of the house is highly irregular in shape, and charmingly so. There are gables of assorted sizes with carved bargeboards, steeply pointed roofs and prominent chimneys. The chimneys were status symbols, for they indicated fireplaces at a time when the poor and the old-fashioned still had open hearths, with holes in the roof for the smoke. There are many large windows, which were another status symbol, because only the rich could afford so much glass. These windows also add to the irregular appearance of the house, since they are of different sizes, while some are flush with the wall and others are bays.

The house is timber-framed, the upper storey being jettied, or overhanging, in some places. The infilling is brick and the roof is covered with tiles. Like other old buildings in the area, Dorney Court shows that these materials can be just as attractive as stone.

There have been alterations and additions to the house, but they have not destroyed the original plan, which was typical of its period.

The most important room was still the great hall, two storeys high and having a roof of open timbers. At one end was a passage, separated from the hall by a screen and with a gallery over it. At the opposite end was a dais, with 'high table' for the owner, his family and important guests. At Dorney the roof had been covered, in part, with plaster while the linenfold panelling and the fireplace came from elsewhere, but, none the less, the hall still has the authentic atmosphere of the original.

Beyond the screens passage of a medieval house was the service area with a pantry, or bread store, a buttery, or wine store, and a kitchen. At Dorney these places are grouped round a small courtyard.

Beyond the dais end of the hall were the private rooms of the owner and his family. Here, there is a parlour on the ground floor with the Great Chamber above it. The parlour fireplace has a splendid wooden overmantel of about 1600. The panelling in the Great Chamber is original.

Visitors also see three bedrooms, with good panelling and fireplaces, and the dining room. The dining room, though it dates from about 1900, is in the William and Mary style, so it is classical and makes a striking contrast with the older interiors. Note particularly the ceilings, the panelling, the fireplaces and the ornament.

Dorney Court houses an excellent collection of furniture as well as a series of portraits representing every one of the twelve generations that have owned the house since 1620. The greatest treasure is, perhaps, an Elizabethen tapestry, known as the Palmer Needlework. In the hall there is a large carving of a pineapple, representing the first ever grown in England. The owner of Dorney Court presented it to Charles II. The king, though, took more than the pineapple, for the lady of the house, Barbara Palmer, became his mistress for some fifteen years. She is best known as the Countess of Castlemaine.

The gardens of Dorney Court are attractive, pleasant places to stroll.

Englefield House.

Englefield House Gardens, Theale, Reading RG7 5EH. Telephone: 0734 302221. Restricted opening times.

Woodland and splendid terraced gardens make the grounds of Englefield House an excellent place for quiet enjoyment.

The house itself is not open to visitors, but there are close views of it from the gardens. It dates from the reign of Elizabeth I but was so badly damaged by fire in 1886 that it had to be largely rebuilt. How much of it is now original Elizabethan work is hard to say, though the entrance tower on the east front is certainly Victorian. Paintings made before the fire show that the house still looks much the same as it always did.

Flints used in the walls have been squared and laid in courses, which is rare for Berkshire.

Savill Garden, The Great Park, Windsor. Telephone: 0753 860222. The garden has set opening times and there is an admission charge.

Savill Garden was begun in 1932. This 35 acre (14 ha) woodland garden offers interest and beauty all the year round, with many varieties of trees, shrubs and woodland plants. In addition there is a more formal area dedicated to herbaceous borders, roses and alpines, and an interesting dry garden. (See also Windsor Great Park, below.)

Stratfield Saye House, Stratfield Saye, Reading RG7 2BT. Telephone: 0256 882882.

Stratfield Saye House was given to the first Duke of Wellington for his services in the wars against Napoleon. It was built in several stages. The first house was on the H plan, but with a very long horizontal stroke. Viewed from the west, that is from near the stables, the original building is the central block and the two inner wings, with their Dutch gables. This dates from about 1630. The two outer wings were added in the eighteenth and nineteenth centuries and also given Dutch gables. The porch dates from 1838 and the cupola from 1964.

On the east front, little of the first house can be seen. Originally, there was the central block and two wings projecting well forward. In 1745 a gallery was built filling almost all the space between the wings. Care was taken to match the new windows with the old, but the classical pediment in the centre contrasts with the Dutch gables on the wings. So far symmetry had been preserved, but in 1775 the dining room with its bay window was added at the north end and, in 1838, the conservatory was built at the south end.

Some of the more striking features of the interior are the Roman mosaics in the hall, which came from Calleva, the unusual coffered ceiling in the library and the Jacobean staircase. There are many mementos of the great Duke, including a lock of hair from the mane of his horse.

The Wellington Exhibition in the stables describes the Duke's career. The many interesting items on display include his huge elaborate funeral carriage.

Swallowfield Park, Swallowfield, Reading. Telephone: 0734 883815. Country Houses Association. Restricted opening.

Various distinguished people have owned Swallowfield Park. One was the second Earl of Clarendon, who acquired it by marrying the heiress to the estate. In 1719 it was bought by Thomas 'Diamond' Pitt, who had been governor of Madras and had used his position to amass a fortune. His most spectacular coup was to buy a hugh rough diamond for £24,000 and sell it, after it had been cut, for £125,000. It was the size of a plum and flawless.

In 1820 Sir Henry Russell bought Swallowfield, and in that same year the authoress Mary Mitford moved with her parents to the neighbouring village of Three Mile Cross (chapter 9). Lady Russell befriended Mary, who in 1851 came to live in Swallowfield village, where she spent her last years.

Dickens's dog also spent its declining years at Swallowfield because the author was friendly with Sir Charles Russell and bequeathed the animal to him.

Swallowfield Park: doorway by Talman.

When the Earl of Clarendon came to Swallowfield he demolished the house which was there and employed Wren's assistant, William Talman, to build a new one. The shell of Talman's house remains, but little else save the oval vestibule on the south side and the beautiful doorway, which has been re-erected in the garden. The Russells remodelled the interior of the house, removing a Grinling Gibbons cornice in the process, added the porte-cochère and covered the outside brick walls with rendering.

The rambling seventeenth-century outbuildings dominate the main house, but they are attractive and are all the more so for having kept their brick finish.

In the grounds there is a pleasing variety of trees and a walled garden.

Valley Gardens, Windsor Great Park. The gardens are freely open at all times during the hours of daylight.

Valley Gardens were begun in 1949. They contain, mainly, trees and shrubs, especially rhododendrons and azaleas, but there are also many wild daffodils. There is a profusion of spring flowers and autumn colour.

Next to Valley Gardens is a heather garden which contains, as well as a splendid collection of heathers, many dwarf conifers. (See also Windsor Great Park, below.)

Windsor Great Park

The Great Park covers 4800 acres (1940 ha), the most attractive part being the southeast corner. This is best explored from either of two car parks. One is next to Savill Garden and is well signposted locally (OS 175: SU 977705). The other is in the park, next to Valley Gardens. It is approached through Cheeseman's Gate, opposite the Bailiwick pub about half a mile (800 metres) south-east of the Savill Garden car park.

It will be useful to have the *Windsor and the Great Park Footpath Map*, available from the Tourist Information Office at Windsor.

Skill and care went into the planning of the Great Park, but the result is not at all contrived. The ground is undulating, there are winding paths through open spaces and woodland, there are ponds and lakes, picturesque views, a marvellous variety of trees and, once in a while, a most pleasant surprise.

Many of the charms of the park are due to George, Duke of Cumberland, who earned the nickname 'Butcher' for his massacre of

Bonnie Prince Charlie's Highlanders after the battle of Culloden in 1746. His military duties done, he became Ranger of Windsor Great Park and used his position to provide jobs for some of his disbanded soldiers. He set them to work landscaping the Great Park under the supervision of the architect Thomas Sandby. Sandby's most spectacular achievement was to turn a swamp into a strikingly beautiful lake, Virginia Water.

During the twentieth century two gardens have been established in the park, Savill Garden and Valley Gardens (see separate entries).

Just south of Savill Garden is an obelisk. The inscription says it was erected by a father grateful to his son for his military success. The father was George II and the son was 'Butcher' Cumberland, but the name 'Culloden' does not appear.

Close to the north-east tip of Virginia Water is an American Indian totem pole. It was carved and brought here to celebrate the centenary of the province of British Columbia.

Everything mentioned so far is signposted in the park and may be visited quite easily by using the car parks mentioned above. Two other items are not signposted and need a little walking to find them. One is the ruins of the Roman temple of Leptis Magna, which the Prince Regent had brought here from Libya early in the nineteenth century. From the totem pole the distance is 2 miles (3 km) return. Follow the east side of Virginia Water to the cascade and from there continue along the south side of the lake for a quarter of a mile (400 metres).

In the middle of the park is an equestrian statue to George III, known as the Copper Horse. It is less than 2 miles (3 km) from the Savill Garden car park. Follow the south-west boundary of the garden and, keeping in the same direction, go through Cumberland Gate. Take to the open country on the left of the road and still continue in the same direction. Soon you will pass Cumberland Lodge, once the home of the Duke of Cumberland. Beyond the house, cross a road and go down a slope with the boundary fence of a wood on the right. Before long, the Copper Horse will come into view, on the horizon. This remarkable monument was erected by George IV 'to the best of fathers'. From it stretches a magnificent avenue, the Long Walk, running 2½ miles (4 km) in a straight line to Windsor Castle.

Windsor Great Park: Wick Pond.

REME Museum, Arborfield: 'Ferret' scout car adapted for recovery work.

6
Museums and galleries

ARBORFIELD
Royal Electrical and Mechanical Engineers' Museum, Corps Secretariat, REME, Isaac Newton Road, Arborfield, Reading RG2 9LN. Telephone: 0734 760421.

The task of the REME is to maintain, recover and repair all the Army's technical equipment, from tanks to dentists' drills. The museum shows the history and work of the corps with the aid of life-sized models, dioramas, exhibitions of equipment and good clear written explanations. There are some unusual items, such as a pair of boots from an equestrian statue of Mussolini.

COOKHAM
Stanley Spencer Gallery, King's Hall, Cookham. Telephone: 0628 781110 (Maidenhead Tourist Information Centre).

The artist Sir Stanley Spencer (1891-1959) lived at Cookham. The gallery, a former Methodist chapel, is devoted entirely to his work. There are paintings, drawings, letters and the pram in which the artist carried his materials.

ETON
Brewhouse Gallery, Eton College, Windsor SL4 6DB. Telephone: 0753 869991.

The gallery houses a changing selection from the College's excellent and varied art collection. This includes watercolours (amongst them a Gainsborough), drawings, engravings, and portraits of Provosts and school leavers.

The gallery also houses the Myers Museum. This is an interesting collection of Egyptian antiquities made by an Old Etonian army officer while serving in Egypt during the late nineteenth century.

Museum of Eton Life, Eton College, Windsor SL4 6DB. Telephone: 0753 869991.

This museum gives a good idea of what it was like to be at Eton in different centuries. The exhibits include early documents, a birch and a diorama of a boy's room of about 1900. There is an entertaining video of life at the College today.

NEWBURY

Newbury District Museum, The Wharf, Newbury RG14 5AS. Telephone: 0635 30511.

The museum is housed in the former Cloth Hall and the adjoining Granary. The Cloth Hall was built in 1626-7 with money bequeathed to the town in 1624 by John Kendrick, to provide a place of work for poor people who would otherwise have been unemployed. As the name suggests, they made woollen cloth. The Granary was built c.1720 as warehousing to serve the Kennet Navigation.

The archaeology section includes an excellent display of the Thatcham Moors settlement. This was on the north bank of the Kennet just east of the town and was one of the most important middle stone age sites in England. The site has since been destroyed by gravel extraction.

The history of Newbury is very well covered and includes a splendid section on the Civil War, with an audio-visual account of the two battles of Newbury. The costume

Newbury District Museum.

gallery is delightful and full of atmosphere. Transport subjects covered include both the Kennet Navigation and ballooning.

READING

Blake's Lock Museum, Gasworks Road, Kenavon Drive, Reading RG1 3DH. Telephone: 0734 390918.

This museum is in part of a nineteenth-century pumping station beside the river Kennet. It concentrates mainly on life in Reading in the nineteenth and twentieth centuries. There are reconstructions of a bakery, a printer's workshop and a men's hairdressing saloon. Exhibits of other trades, retail and manufacturing, include toy bazaars, confectioners, chemists, brickmaking and the making of Cock's famous Reading sauce. An important section covers the history of the local waterways, that is the rivers Thames and Kennet and the Kennet and Avon Canal.

The most spectacular exhibit is a gypsy caravan of 1910.

Museum of English Rural Life, University of Reading, Whiteknights, Reading RG6 2AG. Telephone: 0734 318663. 1½ miles (2.4 km) from the town centre on A327 to Aldershot.

Exhibits cover farm tools, equipment, machinery and rural crafts. The Farmers' Gallery has dioramas of a kitchen, a bakery, a laundry, a dairy and a parlour. There is a splendid collection of wagons.

The Museum of Reading, Town Hall, Blagrave Street, Reading RG1 1QH. Telephone: 0734 399802.

At the time of writing, the museum was closed. It is to be housed in the Victorian town hall, which is being restored. The building, when work is finished, will be spectacular, with an astonishing concert hall containing a 'Father' Willis organ.

When the museum is completed, the largest display will tell the story of Reading from Saxon times to the present day, especially Reading Abbey. All other aspects of local history will be covered, such as archaeology and social and industrial history. There will be a colourful collection of biscuit tins and posters from Huntley and Palmers.

An important section will show finds from *Calleva*, a Romano-British town about 10 miles (16 km) away (chapter 3).

Other sections will deal with costume,

photography (Fox Talbot worked in Reading), geology and natural history. The display on man and his environment from earliest times should be particularly interesting.

The natural history section will have an exploratorium, with video microscopes, and there will be archaeological specimens for children to handle.

Reading has an important collection of fine and decorative art to display in its art gallery.

One of the aims of the new museum is to cater for as wide a public as possible, including toddlers and disabled and blind people. The gallery telling the story of Reading, and including a copy of the Bayeux Tapestry, is expected to open in spring 1993.

RISELEY
National Dairy Museum, Wellington Country Park, Riseley, Reading RG7 1SP. Telephone: 0734 326444.

The museum covers the history of the dairy industry. There are old implements and pieces of equipment for milking and making butter and cheese. They are made from wood, pewter and copper, all being functional, while many are also very attractive. Dairying was the work of the women on the farm, and very arduous it was, especially the handling of heavy cheeses, which needed constant turning after they had been made.

The museum has some vehicles for the delivery of milk, including a delightful little handcart. (See also chapter 7.)

SILCHESTER
Calleva Museum, Sawyers Lands, Silchester, Reading. Telephone: 0734 566226 (Reading Tourist Information Centre).

Although this is a tiny museum, unattended and with few artefacts, it gives admirable explanations of the Roman town of *Calleva*, half a mile (800 metres) away (chapter 3).

SLOUGH
Slough Museum, 23 Bath Road, Slough SL1 3UF. Telephone: 0753 526422.

The museum has two galleries, one of which describes the history of Slough from prehistoric times to the present day, while the other is used for temporary exhibitions.

SULHAMSTEAD
Thames Valley Police Museum, Police Training Centre, Sulhamstead, Reading RG7 4DU. Telephone: 0734 536758. Strictly by appointment, Mondays to Fridays 9 am to 1 pm only; evening visits can be arranged. School and other parties are catered for and research students are most welcome.

The Thames Valley Police Force was formed in 1968 by the amalgamation of the Oxford City, Reading Borough, Berkshire, Buckinghamshire and Oxfordshire forces. The museum deals with the history of these forces since the nineteenth century. The memorabilia shown include charge books, truncheons and relics from the Great Train Robbery.

WINDSOR
Exhibition of The Queen's Presents and Royal Carriages, Windsor Castle, Windsor. Telephone: 0753 831118.

The museum houses several spectacular carriages and many of the gifts which the Queen and the Duke of Edinburgh have received in their travels round the world. The carriages are changed from time to time, but visitors may expect to see an Ascot landau, Queen Victoria's pony cart and a very early charabanc. The presents are amazingly varied. They include a magnificent sword from Saudi Arabia, a Mexican hat, a model of Durham Cathedral, a stock whip from the Australian outback and a silver watering can from India.

Household Cavalry Museum, Combermere Barracks, St Leonards Road, Windsor SL4 3DN. Telephone: 0753 868222 extension 5203.

The museum describes the part the Household Cavalry has played in Britain's wars from Cromwell's day to the Falklands conflict. There are clear explanations, with good battle plans and plenty of material for the serious historian. There are, as well, many fascinating exhibits which everyone will enjoy, such as weapons, uniforms, models and battle souvenirs.

The Courage Shire Horse Centre.

7
Other places to visit

Beale Bird Park, Church Farm, Lower Basildon, Reading RG8 9NH. Telephone: 0734 845172.

The park concentrates mainly on birds, keeping many kinds of waterfowl, parrots, game birds and owls. All are in conditions as near as possible to the wild. As well as resident birds, many wild ones are attracted by the variety of habitats. 125 species have been seen.

In addition to birds, there are larger animals, including some rare breeds. There is a good variety of plants and insects. A tropical house contains fish, birds and insects. Younger children will enjoy the play areas, the paddling pools and the pets' corner. Other attractions include a narrow-gauge railway and the National Centre for Model Ships and Boats. There are river trips in summer, fishing and a craft centre.

Courage Shire Horse Centre, Cherry Garden Lane, Maidenhead Thicket, Maidenhead SL6 3QD. Telephone: 0628 824848.

The Centre has a dozen Shire horses as well as harnesses, brasses and an audio-visual display. Farriers, coopers and a harness-maker can often be seen at work.

There are a playground and a small animal and bird area.

Kennet and Avon Canal
The placid waters of this canal are dangerous. Particular care is needed at locks, which are deep, with sheer sides.

The Kennet and Avon Canal is now open along its entire length from Reading to Bath. In Berkshire it runs from the Thames at Reading through Newbury and Hungerford to the county boundary, the most attractive stretch being west of Newbury.

As pleasant a way as any to enjoy the canal is by walking or cycling along the towpath. It may be reached where roads cross the canal and these places can be found easily on Ordnance Survey Landranger map 174.

For people who want a boat trip, the Kennet and Avon Canal Trust runs a motor barge from Hungerford. Contact the Booking Manager, 7 Manor Park, Froxfield, Wiltshire SN8 3LF (telephone: 0488 683006). The Kennet Horse Boat Company (telephone: 0635 44154) runs a horse-drawn barge eastwards from Kintbury and a motor barge westwards from Newbury. A boat specially adapted for the disabled operates from Hungerford (the Bruce Charitable Trust; telephone: 0488 682277).

Anyone wishing to canoe or take a private boat along the canal should obtain the appropriate leaflet, either *Canoeing* or *Boaters' Information*, from British Waterways, Lower Wharf, Padworth, Reading RG7 4JS (telephone: 0734 712277).

British Waterways produce other useful literature, including a programme of guided walks and leaflets describing two town walks, *The Kennet and Avon Canal in Reading* and *Newbury Discovery Trail*. These publications are on sale at the British Waterways Visitors' Centre at Aldermaston Wharf.

The canal is rich in wildlife. Thirty species of aquatic plants have been recorded, including five water buttercups. There are aquatic insects, such as dragonflies and damselflies, birds such as mallard, moorhens, coots, mute swans and kingfishers, and mammals such as water voles and water shrews. There are many fish but the fishing rights have been leased to clubs.

The plants which grow between the towpath and the canal give shelter to migrants such as the sedge warbler and provide food for butterflies. Hedgerows on the other side of the towpath are a habitat for many species of birds, animals, amphibians and reptiles.

Lambourn Trainers' Association, Seven Barrows, Lambourn, RG16 7UJ. Telephone: 0488 72664.

It is essential to make an appointment. Wear shoes suitable for walking in grass.

The Association's members give guided tours, lasting up to two hours. Visitors see the stables, where they watch the training of racehorses and look at the individual animals. A horse may be turned loose in a corral, to show its paces. Visitors are also taken to see the gallops and are shown around the stable yard.

Magna Carta Island, Wraysbury.

It was here that rebellious barons forced King John to accept Magna Carta in June 1215. The island in the Thames is in private occupation and there is no access to it, but nearby there are the Magna Carta Memorial, two National Trust car parks, a large play area and a restaurant on the south side of the river. Boats run from here.

On the other side of the road are the RAF and Kennedy memorials.

Monkey Island: the former 'fishing temple', now part of a hotel.

Monkey Island, Bray, Maidenhead SL6 2EE. Telephone (hotel): 0628 23400.

In 1723 this island was bought by the third Duke of Marlborough, who erected two buildings on it known as a 'fishing lodge' and a 'fishing temple'. Today these buildings are Monkey Island Hotel.

The island is reached by a footbridge. The temple is on the right and the lodge is on the left. In the lodge there is a ceiling painted with monkeys, dressed in human costume and enjoying themselves hunting, fishing and boating. This is the work of the eighteenth-century French artist Andie de Clermont. Anyone who patronises the hotel bar may see the monkeys, for they are in the room next door.

This was Monkey Island long before Clermont painted his ceiling. In the middle ages it was known as 'Monks Eyot' and belonged to Merton Priory.

Royalty and Empire, Windsor and Eton Central Station, Thames Street, Windsor SL4 1PJ. Telephone: 0753 857837.

In 1897, the year of Queen Victoria's Diamond Jubilee, the Great Western Railway built a new station at Windsor. During the celebrations the Royal Family and their more distinguished guests stayed at Windsor, travelling to and from London by train. In the station today there is an exhibition by Madame Tussaud's, showing the arrival of the royal train from Paddington.

The Thames

Many people have drowned in the Thames. Treat it with respect.

The river may be enjoyed by boat or by walking along the towpath.

Several firms run passenger boats, including Salter Brothers (Folly Bridge, Oxford OX1 4LA; telephone: 0865 243421) and tourist information centres can supply details of other companies operating from Windsor, Reading and elsewhere. There are firms offering boats and cruisers for hire by the day and longer at Reading, Wargrave, Cookham, Maidenhead and Runnymede. Again, tourist information centres will have information, or bookings can be made through the Thames Hire Cruiser Association (19 Acre End Street, Eynsham, Oxford OX8 1PE; telephone: 0865 880107).

For walks along the towpath, see chapter 2.

Royalty and Empire exhibition by Madame Tussaud's at Windsor station: Queen Victoria leaves the royal waiting room with the 2nd Battalion of the Coldstream Guards as Guard of Honour.

Wellington Country Park.

Thames Valley Vineyard, Stanlake Park, Twyford, Reading RG10 0BN. Telephone: 0734 340176.

The vineyard produces ten types of wine, six whites, two sparkling and two reds. These wines have won many awards in national and international competitions. Output is up to 100,000 bottles a year. Individual visitors may taste wines and there are conducted tours for groups by appointment. A viewing area overlooks the winery installed within a Cromwellian barn.

The vineyard is in the grounds of Stanlake Park, a late sixteenth-century house, which may be glimpsed from the winery. It is not open to the public.

Wellington Country Park, Riseley, Reading RG7 1SP. Telephone: 0734 326444; for water sports ring 0734 326505, and for the riding school 0734 326308.

Here there are lakes, a deer park, a children's animal farm, nature trails and the National Dairy Museum (see chapter 6).

The park offers a variety of activities, including fishing, boating, an adventure playground, a miniature railway and crazy golf. Beside the park is a riding school.

Westbury Farm Fishery and Vineyard, Purley-on-Thames, Reading RG8 8DL. Telephone: 0734 843123.

The vineyard, of 16 acres (6.5 ha), produces seventeen white wines, three reds and a rosé. Output is as much as 100,000 bottles a year. There are conducted tours for groups.

There are two attractive lakes for fishing. Visitors wanting to fish should telephone to make a booking.

Windsor Brass Rubbing Centre, St John the Baptist's Church, High Street, Windsor. Telephone: 0753 852730 (after 6 pm).

This is a splendid place for brass rubbing, for there are replicas of one hundred brasses. The most popular is that of Margaret Bernard Peyton, known as the 'lace lady' on account of her pretty dress. The oldest is the brass of Sir Robert de Bures, which dates from about 1300. The centre can supply an information sheet for every one of its brasses, giving its place, its date and a history of the family.

Windsor Safari Park, Winkfield Road, Windsor SL4 4AY. Telephone: 0753 830886. The entrance price includes admission to all the shows and attractions.

Visitors to Windsor Safari Park can enjoy an African Adventure and explore the Egyptian Entrance and Moroccan Village. Safari Roadtrains take them close to the wild animals and a funicular railway passes the Elephant Gardens. Other attractions include the Seaworld Show, the Birds of Prey display and the Port Livingstone area, which includes the Limpopo Crocodiles, Swamp Devils and the African Queen Riverboat Ride.

Windsor Castle.

8

Windsor Castle and Eton College

WINDSOR CASTLE

Telephone: 0753 831118.

Windsor Castle has a history as a fortress, a royal palace and a religious foundation.

The fortress

Covering 13 acres (5.3 ha), Windsor is the largest castle in England. It is in an excellent defensive position, for it stands on an isolated chalk outcrop 100 feet (30 metres) high, with a precipice on the north side.

The first castle here was built by William the Conqueror. Like most early Norman castles, it had a motte and a bailey, both of earth. A motte was like an inverted pudding bowl, being roughly circular, with a flat top, while baileys were lower but had no standard shape. The one at Windsor was divided into three wards, the Upper, the Middle and the Lower. Wooden stockades crowned both the motte and the bailey while the buildings inside the defences were also of wood.

The castle was protected by a ditch, save on the north side where the precipice made it unnecessary. There was also a ditch separating the Lower and Middle Wards.

In 1165 Henry II began the rebuilding of the castle in stone and this work was completed in the thirteenth century, under Henry III. The later defences are around the Lower Ward. They have powerful drum towers, typical of this period when castles were at their strongest.

By the sixteenth century the main gateway was in ruins, so Henry VIII replaced it with the one which bears his name.

King John stayed at Windsor during the Magna Carta negotiations of 1215 and at night showed his feelings by rolling on the floor, biting the straw which covered it and clawing the air. In 1216 he rejected the charter and this led to a war with the barons. They besieged Windsor for three months, but John's Constable, Engelond de Cicogné, defended it successfully. This was the only serious attack ever made on the castle.

Early in the nineteenth century George IV employed Jeffry Wyatville to transform Windsor from a workmanlike castle into a romantic one. Wyatville did so by raising the height of many of the walls and towers and adding touches such as false portcullis grooves and machicolation. All this has been described as 'toy-town' architecture.

The palace

The Saxon kings had a hunting lodge at Old Windsor, but the Norman kings moved into their new castle. Henry II rebuilt the living quarters in stone, as he did the defences. The palace was extended several times during the middle ages.

The medieval building stood until Charles II employed Hugh May to demolish most of it and build a new palace in the baroque style. At the same time the grounds were improved, for example by extending the terraces and planting the Long Walk.

Windsor was neglected for much of the eighteenth century, so it fell into decay. Then, in 1796, George III employed James Wyatt to repair and remodel the palace. The work continued under George IV, his architect being James Wyatt's nephew, Jeffry Wyatville.

We have already seen that Wyatville made important changes to the castle. His alterations to the palace were even more drastic. He added a great deal, including an extra storey, modified many of the rooms and 'gothicised' the exterior.

Reactions to Wyatville's work were mixed. Thomas Creevey said: 'All the New Rooms make a very good Gentleman's or Nobleman's house, Nothing more.' Certainly the palace was a labyrinth. There are several stories of guests who were unable to find their rooms. The French historian Guizot barged into Queen Victoria's dressing room and another visitor had to spend the night on a couch in the State Gallery. Further, while he was concentrating on his architecture, Wyatville was neglecting the drains. That may well have led to Prince Albert's death from typhoid in 1861.

The religious foundation

The religious foundation at Windsor was linked to the Order of the Garter. Both date from 1348. According to a story written a hundred years after the event, Edward III was dancing with the delectable Countess of Salisbury when her garter fell to the ground. As the courtiers mocked, Edward put the garter on his own leg, saying *'Honi soit qui mal y pense'* ('Dishonoured be he who thinks ill of it' or, more succinctly, if less accurately, 'Evil to him who evil thinks'). In some way, which is not at all clear, this is supposed to have led to the formation of the Order of the Garter, with the king's remark as its motto.

There were twenty-four Knights of the Garter, but the order was religious as well as military. Whenever a knight died, one thousand masses were to be said for his soul, which would have made intolerable demands on his fellows. Accordingly, the masses were said by a college of a dean, twelve canons, twelve priest-vicars and twenty-four poor knights. At first the college used the existing chapel in the castle but at the end of the fifteenth century St George's Chapel was built for it.

The Lower Ward

Visitors come through the Henry VIII Gateway into the Lower Ward.

Opposite the gateway is a brick and timber-framed range of buildings with an entrance to the Horseshoe Cloister. This cloister was built in about 1480 for the priest-vicars. It owes its nineteenth-century appearance to Gilbert Scott, who restored it heavily in 1871. The wide staircase leading to the west door of St George's Chapel is also by Scott.

Plan of Windsor Castle in Norman times.

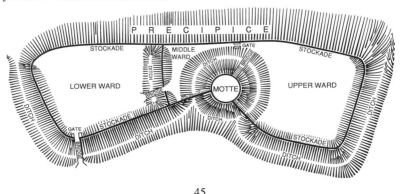

Windsor Castle: St George's Chapel.

In the north-west corner of the castle is the Curfew Tower, one of the powerful drum towers built in the reign of Henry III. The walls of its basement are 13 feet (4 metres) thick. The conical roof, with a French look, was added in 1863. From the main floor there is a passage that once led to a sally port. In the tower are the bells of St George's Chapel, which chime every three hours.

Facing St George's Chapel and built against the south wall of the Lower Ward are the lodgings of the Military Knights. They are the successors of the Poor Knights and were given their more dignified title by William IV in 1833.

St George's Chapel

St George's Chapel is in the Perpendicular style throughout and is one of the most splendid examples of its period, though it is by no means typical. There is a transept halfway along the building, which makes the nave and the chancel equal in length, each being of seven bays. Such symmetry is unusual in a Gothic building but probably there was no conscious attempt to achieve it. It is more likely that the chapel had a long chancel simply because it was served by a large college of priests. In any event, the two halves of the building are not identical because the east and west polygonal chapels are positioned differently in relation to the end bays, are of different heights and have different roofs. The transept has a polygonal end, which is unusual.

Flying buttresses take the weight of the vaulting. Above them are pinnacles, capped with figures known as the King's Beasts. They are carvings of animals which kings have taken as their emblems, for example the white hart of Richard II. Sir Christopher Wren had the original beasts taken down to reduce weight on the building, but they were replaced in 1930.

Inside, the nave arcades have high slender columns with four-centred arches. They are decorated with continuous mouldings, which means that the columns have no capitals. The nave vault has a level ceiling in the centre with coving on either side. The ceiling is a marvel, with the ribs forming stars, and, covering the joints, a bewildering variety of bosses. The coving is a series of vaults. Between 1921 and 1930 all the vaults in the chapel were taken down and rebuilt, at which time some alarming examples of medieval jerry-building were found.

There are several interesting monuments in the nave and its aisles, but, artistically, the most striking is Princess Charlotte's, which is in the north-west chapel. The only daughter of George IV, Charlotte died in 1817, having had a stillborn child.

At the east end of the north chancel aisle is a monument to the founder of St George's, Edward IV, and his queen, Elizabeth Woodville.

The chancel is entered through its north door. Immediately on the left is a wrought iron grille which once protected the tomb of Edward IV. There can be no finer piece of craftsmanship in wrought iron than this. It was the work of Henry VII's chief smith, John Tresilian.

On the north wall of the chancel, at the east end, are two oriel windows which light what was once a chantry chapel and is now the Royal Pew.

In the floor of the chancel are the covers to the Royal Vault and a tomb shared by Henry VIII and Charles I. When Charles was interred, a Cromwellian soldier stole one of Henry's bones, meaning to haft a knife with it.

The main interest in the chancel is the stalls. They have three tiers. The upper tier is for the Knights of the Garter and the senior clergy, the middle tier is for the Military Knights and the junior clergy and the lower tier is for the choir. Over each stall belonging to a Knight of the Garter is the man's helmet, with its crest, and his banner, bearing his coat of arms. Every Knight of the Garter has fixed a plate bearing his coat of arms on the back of his stall, so there are now some seven hundred of them.

The carvings on the stalls may not be of the highest quality, but they are full of interest.

On leaving the chancel by the west door, The Queen's desk is on the left and the Prince of Wales's is on the right. The sovereign's misericord has a carving which shows Edward IV and Louis XI of France signing the Treaty of Picquigny in 1475. It was this agreement which marked the end of the Hundred Years' War. The misericord cannot be seen, but there is a replica of it under the organ loft, just outside the chancel.

This end of the chancel is the best place to admire the west window. It contains the figures of 75 popes, kings, princes and saints, all but nine of which date from the early sixteenth century.

In the south chancel aisle, on the left, are four paintings, known as the Panel of Kings. Among them is Edward V, one of the princes murdered in the Tower of London. He was deposed before his coronation could take place, so his crown is shown hovering over his head. Beyond these paintings and also on the left is the sword of Edward III, which is over 2 metres (6 feet 6 inches) long.

Close to the high altar is the tomb of Henry VI. Miracles took place here, so large numbers of pilgrims arrived and the tomb became one of the main sources of income for St George's. The splendid wrought iron almsbox nearby was probably for the pilgrims' offerings. It is ironic that Henry's remains should have enriched a chapel built by the man who deposed and murdered him, while his own foundation, Eton, which is just across the river, was short of money.

There was another lucrative shrine for St George's in the south-east chapel, where pilgrims also came to be cured. It contained the body of John Schorn, rector of North Marston in Buckinghamshire. He was said to have conjured the Devil into a boot, though for what reason is not clear. At the Reformation such beliefs were dismissed as superstitions and in the 1580s the Earl of Lincoln appropriated Schorn's chapel. Lincoln lies there with his third wife.

The north-east door of St George's leads into the Dean's Cloister. Round it is a stone bench with holes used for a medieval game. On the south side is a late thirteenth-century painting of the head of a king, all that remains of a fresco. The cloister arcades are fourteenth-century. On the north side is a passage leading to the Canons' Cloister, also fourteenth-century.

An opening in the south-west corner of the Dean's Cloister leads to the antechapel of the Albert Memorial Chapel. Here, there is another painting of a king's head, also thirteenth-century.

The Albert Memorial Chapel is on the site of a chapel built in the thirteenth century and which the Garter Knights used until 1483. Soon after that, it was rebuilt as a Lady Chapel for St George's. When Prince Albert died, Queen Victoria appropriated it as a memorial for him. Marble panels with pictures etched on them were put round the walls and the ceiling was covered with mosaics. Later, much of the floor space was occupied by a monument to the Duke of Clarence.

The Middle Ward and the Round Tower

To the east of the Albert Memorial Chapel is the Deanery. Christopher Wren lived here as a boy, for his father was Dean of Windsor. The Deanery has a sunken courtyard, all that remains of the ditch that once separated the Lower and Middle Wards.

Much of the Middle Ward is filled by the Norman motte, crowned with the Round Tower. The tower was built by Henry II to replace a wooden stockade. This type of fortification is known as a 'shell keep', for it is just a wall with, originally, lean-to buildings against its inner side. Formerly, the tower was only 30 feet (9 metres) high, but Jeffry Wyatville added another 30 feet. He had greatly increased the height of the buildings in the Upper Ward so he needed to keep the Round Tower in proportion.

Hanging in the tower is the Sebastopol Bell, captured during the Crimean War. It is tolled only on the death of a sovereign.

Queen Mary's Dolls' House

The dolls' house was given to George V's consort in 1923. It measures 8 feet 4 inches (254 cm) by 5 feet 2 inches (157 cm) and is on a scale of one inch to one foot (1:12). It was designed by the architect Edwin Lutyens. The house is already an interesting historical record and, as it is unlikely to be modernised, will become increasingly so.

The State Apartments

The works of art in the State Apartments are changed from time to time, so visitors wishing to study them will need an up-to-date list. It is on sale in the Castle.

The State Apartments still contain walls from the medieval building, though they are not evident. Much more remains of Charles II's palace, which was built round two courtyards. Considerately, the king gave the rooms on the south side to his Portuguese wife, Catherine of Braganza, and took the ones on the north for himself. Jeffry Wyatville altered the queen's rooms so that they could be used for ceremonies, converted the king's rooms into a suite for visiting rulers and moved the sovereign's private quarters to wings on the east and south sides of the Upper Ward.

The Grand Staircase was a late addition to the palace, for it was built by Anthony Salvin in 1866. He was able to make it wide and imposing by putting it in one of Charles II's courtyards. On it is a suit of armour which belonged to Henry VIII in his later and more corpulent years.

The Grand Vestibule has fan vaulting by James Wyatt. Among the exhibits is the bullet which killed Nelson.

The large gloomy Waterloo Chamber is in the second of the original courtyards. It was meant for the portraits of some of the soldiers, statesmen and rulers who had helped defeat Napoleon, but banquets, concerts and plays were also held in it. There are carved panels and foliage hangings, the work of Grinling Gibbons, which were saved from Charles II's palace.

The Garter Throne Room is used for the private ceremonies of the Order. It was once two rooms, as is shown by the arch part of the way along it. The walls date from the twelfth century, though there is no hint of that. Again, there are some superb carvings by Gibbons, notably over the fireplace.

The Grand Reception Room was Charles II's guard room. Following his experiences during the Civil War and his exile, the king was concerned for his own safety. One of his locks fired a bullet if anyone tried to open it with the wrong key. George IV, who lived in more peaceful times, used this room to greet visitors who were going to a function in the Waterloo Chamber. On the walls are six Gobelins tapestries of the late eighteenth century, telling the story of Jason and the Golden Fleece.

St George's Hall has fourteenth-century walls. It was made from the medieval banqueting hall and Charles II's baroque chapel. Here, the Knights of the Garter have their annual banquet. From time to time important state banquets are held here.

The Queen's Guard Chamber was kept by George IV as a military museum. The figure on horseback represents the King's Champion. At a coronation, his duty was to challenge to single combat anyone who dared question the right of the new sovereign to the throne. This particular suit of armour was made for Queen Elizabeth's champion, Sir Christopher Hatton. He was later also her Lord Chancellor and was known as the 'dancing Chancellor' because, it was said, he owed his promotion to his skill in that art.

The Queen's Presence Chamber was where visitors waited for an audience. The ceiling, by Antonio Verrio, shows Queen Catherine under a canopy spread by Time and surrounded by Virtues. Meanwhile, Justice is dealing harshly with the Vices. Pevsner remarks that Verrio's work 'lacks sparkle, let alone brio'. On the other hand, there are more of Gibbons's carvings, which are beyond praise. The tapestries, again Gobelins of the late eighteenth century, tell the Bible story of King Ahasuerus and Queen Esther.

The Queen's Audience Chamber was where visitors were received. The Verrio ceiling shows Catherine drawn by swans to the Temple of Virtue.

The Queen's Ball Room was built as the nursery wing by Edward III in the fourteenth century. The chandeliers are from the time of George III.

The Queen's Drawing Room was her 'withdrawing room', where she could escape from the King's Dining Room and her own Audience Chamber.

We now come to the rooms set aside for the king in the time of Charles II. The King's Closet was his private sitting room and the King's Dressing Room was, in spite of its name, where he slept.

The State Bedroom was indeed a bedroom for a time, but more and more Charles II brought people here for private discussions, so in the end he used it entirely for meetings. The state bed remained, but just as an ornament. Under George IV the room once again became a bedroom, though for visiting dignitaries. The bed, which is French and eighteenth-century, was put here by Queen Victoria for the Empress Eugénie, who came to England with Napoleon III in 1855.

The King's Drawing Room served the same purposes as the Queen's.

The King's Dining Room has a Verrio ceiling, the Banquet of the Gods. Yet again there are carvings by Gibbons, and as superb as ever. Some of the royal meals were ceremonies which members of the public were allowed to attend, though only as spectators. The event might have been very different from feeding time at the zoo, but the principle was the same.

The Upper Ward

Most of the Upper Ward must be viewed through iron railings. This area, 375 feet (114 metres) by 230 feet (70 metres), is known as the Quadrangle. The north range, with the porte-cochère, contains the State Apartments while the two other ranges contain the Private Apartments.

Most of what we see is the work of Jeffry Wyatville, whose aim was to restore the Gothic character which the palace had lost when Charles II rebuilt it in the baroque style. This 'gothicisation' shows in the battlements and turrets, the entrances of different shapes and sizes, the pointed arches and the bay and oriel windows. The result, though, does not look authentic and the main reason is the windows. In many places they are spaced regularly and where this happens there is also a low proportion of window to wall. Both features are in the classical rather than the Gothic tradition.

In the Quadrangle is a splendid statue of Charles II with carving by Grinling Gibbons on its pedestal.

Dividing the Upper and Middle Wards is the Norman Gateway, which, in spite of its name, was built in 1359. Formerly it was a state prison. Distinguished captives at Windsor included David II of Scotland, taken at Neville's Cross in 1346, King John of France, taken at Poitiers in 1356, and King James I of Scotland, taken at sea in 1413. During his stay of eleven years, James was made a Knight of the Garter. Moreover, he met, fell in love with and married Lady Joan Beaufort.

FROGMORE HOUSE

Frogmore House, Home Park, Windsor. Telephone: 0753 868286. Access is from the car park at its south-east corner. From Windsor, take A308 towards Staines and follow the signposts to the house.

Frogmore began as a fairly modest manor house, built in the early eighteenth century, but in the 1790s George III employed James Wyatt to enlarge it. George wanted a quiet retreat for Queen Charlotte and a place of confinement for his daughters. Even though he and his wife were happily married, they were determined that the princesses should remain single so that they could devote themselves to their parents.

In Victoria's reign Frogmore became the home of her mother, the Duchess of Kent.

During the late nineteenth and early twentieth centuries, Frogmore's royal owners neglected it so badly that there was talk of demolishing it. However, George V's consort, Queen Mary, needed somewhere to keep her gifts and decided Frogmore was the place. The house survived as a trinket box until the 1980s, when it was lavishly restored and refurnished at the taxpayers' expense.

The original manor house was of seven

bays and two storeys. James Wyatt added a third storey, two wings and a loggia. In the early nineteenth century the wings were enlarged by adding bow-fronted pavilions and, at some unknown date, the arcade of the loggia was glazed.

Many of the rooms are spectacular, but perhaps the most appealing is the one which Mary Moser decorated with flowers. Gloomy colours had been daubed over them, but that paint has been carefully removed and the flowers are now as bright as they ever were.

Frogmore's delightful gardens were laid out in the 1790s. There is no access to the gardens of the Royal Mausoleum (see Windsor, chapter 9). These are open on two days in May and access is from the Long Walk on the other side of Home Park. For information telephone: 0753 868286.

Plan of the centre of Windsor and Eton, showing principal features referred to in this chapter.

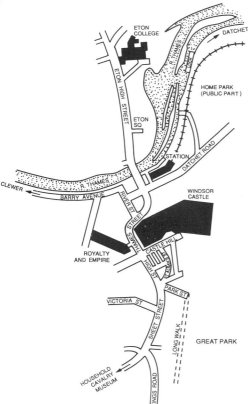

ETON COLLEGE

Eton College, Windsor SL4 6DB. Telephone: 0753 869991.

History

In 1440 Henry VI founded Eton College, and in 1441 its partner, King's College, Cambridge. The full name of the former was 'The Provost and Royal College of Blessed Mary of Eton by Windsor'. There were to be 'a Provost, ten priests, four clerks, six choristers, twenty-five poor scholars to learn grammar and twenty-five poor men, with a master to teach the scholars and any other boys coming from any part of England, free of charge'. The foundation was called a college because it was, essentially, a religious community, though it had attached to it a school and almshouses. 'Grammar' meant the classics, which had a practical value in the middle ages, when Latin was the common language of all educated Europeans and was essential for entry to the professions.

The founder's original ideas were modified. Indeed, the plan for the almshouses was scrapped almost at once and the number of scholars was increased to seventy. Today, the college of priests and clerks is no more, though the post of Provost survives as head of the governing body. The seventy poor scholars educated free of charge are now about 1270 pupils, most of them with wealthy parents and paying substantial fees. There are indeed seventy King's Scholars, the successors of Henry VI's. Many of them are still educated completely free, and others benefit from scholarships and bursaries that cover a substantial proportion of the fees.

From the beginning, Eton admitted more boys than the seventy King's Scholars, but while scholars lived in the main college, as they still do, the others had to live in the town. They are known as Oppidans. At first the Oppidans lodged in inns or with families, but, later, houses were established specially for them. The houses and other college buildings now form quite a large settlement. They are of all periods and styles, the most interesting being in the streets and alleys near the college.

Instead of a single master there are now almost 140, while ancillary members of staff abound. The staff congregates in the hall once a day, to exchange information and hear the Head Master's announcements. Any boy wishing to see a master will wait for him outside and then, to attract his attention, will

The playing fields of Eton.

seize the arm of his gown.

Public school education reached its nadir in the eighteenth and early nineteenth centuries. Gladstone, who was at Eton from 1821 to 1827, described it as 'the greatest pagan school in Christendom'. The scholars had poor food, they washed at the pump and they slept in damp dormitories. They were under no sort of control during much of the day. If Wellington did indeed say that Waterloo was won on the playing fields of Eton, he could not have been referring to organised games, for there were none. He meant fights. The son of the Earl of Shaftesbury, Anthony Ashley Francis Cooper, was killed in one of these in 1825. At eight o' clock in the evening scholars of all ages were locked into the Long Chamber and left to their own devices. One sport was for the older boys to run races on the backs of the younger ones, which they did wearing spurs.

Staff were almost as barbaric. The diminutive John Keate, headmaster from 1809 to 1834, would flog as many as eighty boys in a day. Once, he found a group of boys outside his study and, without asking questions, flogged them all. He then remembered that they were his divinity class. The floggings were with the birch, which drew blood and left pieces of twig embedded in the flesh.

Well into the nineteenth century, the classics were the only subjects of importance in the curriculum, and they remained pre-eminent into the early twentieth century.

Eton became fairly humane after Dr Hawtrey was appointed headmaster in 1853, and eventually the curriculum was widened. It is now thoroughly modern.

Buildings

The main entrance to the College leads into School Yard. From here, it is possible to follow the original plan, which had just three parts. They were the chapel to the south, the cloisters, entered through the imposing brick tower, to the east and the school to the north.

In the centre of School Yard is a statue of Henry VI by Francis Bird, 1719. Henry was only an infant when, in 1422, he succeeded his warlike father, Henry V. He grew up into a quiet scholarly man, but suffered intermittently from mental illness after 1453. He was deposed in 1461 by Edward, Duke of York, who became King Edward IV. Warwick the Kingmaker restored Henry in 1470, but Edward IV regained the throne the following year. He had Henry murdered in the Tower of London. On the anniversary of Henry's birth, 6th December, a wreath of bay leaves is placed around his statue in School Yard.

51

Eton College: School Yard and Lupton's Tower.

Eton College chapel.

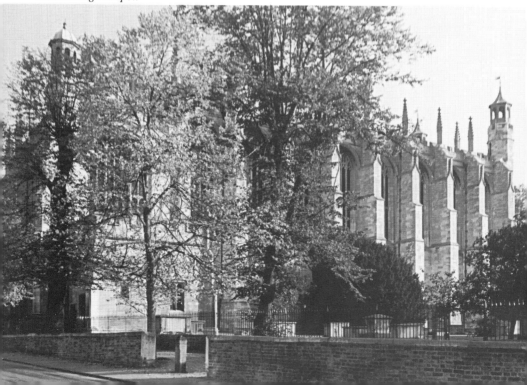

The original schoolroom, still used for teaching, is now known as Lower School. Above it on the first floor was the notorious Long Chamber. The room where the Head Master both lived and worked was on the ground floor at the west end. At the east end was the room of his only assistant, the Usher. The whole school then consisted of just four rooms.

The range which fronts the street, with the open arcade, is Upper School. It was added in the late seventeenth century.

The chapel was built between 1441 and 1482, so it is in the Perpendicular style. There are large windows, strengthened with transoms, massive buttresses capped with pinnacles, and parapets in the form of battlements. The interior is light and spacious.

The chapel was to have had a choir and a nave, but the founder's death halted the work, and William Wayneflete (Provost 1442-7) closed off the choir with an antechapel, finished around 1480.

The chapel floor is several feet above ground level, as a precaution against flooding. The College Hall, entered from the cloisters, is also raised, perhaps for the same reason, but the school has no such protection!

The interior of the chapel has more nineteenth- and twentieth-century work than is, perhaps, good for it. The stalls date from the restoration in 1844, while the screen and the vast organ sitting on it are of the 1880s. The east window, designed by Evie Hone, was given its vivid glass just after the Second World War, during which the previous window was destroyed by a bomb. The three windows nearest the altar on either side were designed by John Piper. The roof was built in 1956, when the existing wooden roof had to be replaced because of dry rot. At a first glance it looks like a medieval fan vault but is much simpler. It is even more different in construction, for it is made of stone-faced concrete panels, suspended from steel girders. The architect was William Holford, who designed the precincts of St Paul's Cathedral.

In the north-east of the chapel is the chantry of Roger Lupton, built in about 1515. It has a fan vault with a pendant and is separated from the choir by a stone screen. Lupton was one of Eton's most famous Provosts, responsible, as we shall see, for some important buildings. West of Lupton's chantry is the Memorial Chapel.

In the antechapel is a statue of Henry VI made by John Bacon in 1786. There are several good monuments in the main chapel, including Provost Murray's, north of the altar. The most striking feature of the chapel interior, though, is the paintings on the walls of the west bays. They were executed in the 1480s but covered with whitewash at the Reformation. They were uncovered in the restoration of the 1840s, when the top strips were destroyed, and were hidden again by stalls until 1923. They were restored in the 1960s. The lower strip on the south side tells the story of an empress, while the north side shows miracles of the Virgin.

The west range of the cloisters, facing School Yard, was built in about 1520. It was the work of Provost Lupton and the splendid entrance tower is named after him. It is four storeys high, with an oriel window lighting two of them. On the corners of the tower are polygonal turrets, five storeys high, which end in lanterns, with cupolas.

The other three ranges of the cloisters were started in 1441 and may have been finished by 1461, when Henry VI was deposed. College Hall, where the King's Scholars eat their meals, is on the south side. The eighteenth-century library is in front of it, and the second and upper storeys of the north and east ranges are of the same period.

North of School Yard and the cloisters are the original playing fields. The Wall Game is played against the far boundary, which runs along the Slough road. This takes place on 30th November each year.

East of the chapel is the Brewhouse Yard, with the brewhouse of 1714. The college museums are here (chapter 6).

In front of the main entrance to the College is an iron street lamp of 1864 known as the Burning Bush. On the other side of the road are the school library and another school hall, both opened in 1908 as memorials to Etonians who died in the Boer War. The library is an imitation of the Radcliffe Camera at Oxford, though it is much more ornate.

Ufton Court near Aldermaston.

9
Towns and villages

ALDERMASTON

The Atomic Weapons Establishment is in the grounds of Aldermaston Court, so there have been demonstrations by the Campaign for Nuclear Disarmament here.

The village street is lined with brick buildings of different ages and styles, but all blending happily. The seventeenth-century lodges of Aldermaston Court, with their Dutch gables, look down the street; the imposing eighteenth-century Hind's Head looks up it. Behind the inn, a few yards along the main road, is a tiny lock-up, last used in 1865, when an inmate burnt to death. On the south side of the church, near the chancel, is the tomb of John Stair, who developed the William pear.

In Aldermaston is a piece of land belonging to the church and known as Church Acre. Every three years this is let by candle auction. A pin is stuck in the side of a tallow candle, the candle is lit and whoever makes the last bid before the pin falls takes the land. There can be no argument about when the pin falls, because it is a horseshoe nail which lands in the tray of the candlestick with a clatter. Candle auctions have given rise to the expression 'You could have heard a pin drop'.

2 miles (3 km) along the A340, towards Reading, is **Aldermaston Wharf**. Here there are an impressive canal basin and a lock, both restored in 1983. There is also a British Waterways Visitors' Centre, which provides information and sells a good selection of books and leaflets.

1½ miles (2.4 km) from Aldermaston Wharf, as the crow flies, is **Ufton Court** (OS 175: SU 626667). It is not open to visitors, but as its drive is a public bridleway it is possible to view it from the outside. This delightful house was built in the reign of Elizabeth I though, with its timber framing and its fourteen gables of assorted sizes, it is more in the style of the early Tudor period.

An eighteenth-century owner of Ufton Court, Francis Perkins, married Arabella Fermor, who was the Belinda of Pope's *Rape of the Lock*. Arabella was famed for her beauty. Pope wrote:

If to her lot some female errors fall
Look on her face and you'll forget 'em all.

ASCOT

Ascot was unimportant until Queen Anne moved the Windsor race meeting here in 1711, and even then little happened until the Duke of Cumberland established a stud at Windsor in the middle of the eighteenth century. By the end of the century the Royal family was attending the races regularly.

Before the Second World War the Royal Ascot Hotel was run by John Fothergill. He came from Thame in Oxfordshire, where he had turned the Spread Eagle into what he termed 'an Eton of public houses', attracting guests like Evelyn Waugh and Augustus John. Fothergill was brilliant at every aspect of his profession save making money, so he failed at Ascot as he had done, financially, at Thame.

To the west of the racecourse and lining the A332 to Windsor are some handsome Victorian and Edwardian villas, but the main attraction of Ascot is the racecourse itself, although it has no buildings of note. The Royal Ascot meeting takes place during the third week in June. For details of race meetings contact The Secretary, Ascot Authority, Grandstand, Ascot (telephone: 0990 22211, 22212 or 22213).

BINFIELD

Alexander Pope spent his boyhood at Binfield, for his family moved to the village after his father, a linen draper, had made his fortune in London. It was here that Pope wrote *The Pastorals*, *An Essay on Criticism* and *The Rape of the Lock*. The Popes' house is in Murrell Hill Lane at OS 175: SU 843697.

The home of Alexander Pope at Binfield.

Five bays wide and three storeys high, it hardly answers the poet's description:

A little house, with trees a-row,
And like its master, very low.

Amen Corner at Binfield has this name because the congregation of a nearby chapel used to disperse with the words 'God be with you, Amen'.

BOXFORD

The village lies in the valley of the Lambourn, 4 miles (6 km) north-west of Newbury. Anyone who admires good thatching should come here, for the place has some splendid roofs. There are two good groups of cottages, one by the church and the other in the hamlet of Westbrook, on the far side of the river Lambourn. A timber-framed house in Westbrook is of cruck construction. The crucks are long curved timbers rising from the ground forming, with the tiebeam, a shape like a capital A with curved sides.

In the late seventeenth century a Quaker called Oliver Sansom lived in the village and feuded with the vicar. When the church tower collapsed into his garden, Sansom kept the rubble, saying it was a gift from Heaven. But it was the vicar who triumphed in the end. He had Sansom jailed for not attending church.

BRACKNELL

Writing in 1949, John Betjeman stigmatised Bracknell as 'the dullest looking town in Berkshire'. That same year, though, it was designated a new town and has changed completely, growing in size and importance. The headquarters of many important companies are here, as well as the Meteorological Office and the Royal Air Force Staff College.

The architecture, much of it of the 1960s, is no longer in vogue, but visitors will find many good shops. There are also some excellent amenities, such as sports centres and swimming pools.

South Hill Park, a house of 1760, is now an arts centre, and beside it is the Wilde Theatre (South Hill Park, Bracknell RG12 4PA; telephone: 0344 427272).

(See also Easthampstead church, chapter 4; The Look Out, chapter 2 and Caesar's Camp, chapter 3.)

BRADFIELD

The village is in the valley of the little river Pang, some 6 or 7 miles (10-11 km) west of the centre of Reading.

There are some attractive cottages by a

Brass in Bray church.

Bray: Jesus Hospital.

stream, an old mill with a weir and three fine Georgian houses. One of these is north-west of the church while the two others are close by in the village street. The village, though, is dominated by its church and a public school, Bradfield College, both the work of the Reverend Thomas Stevens, squire and rector in the middle of the nineteenth century. Stevens thought the medieval church unworthy of him, so he employed Gilbert Scott to rebuild it. He then founded Bradfield College, partly to supply the church with choristers.

BRAY

Bray stands beside the Thames, just south of Maidenhead. The church, St Michael and All Angels, has a nave and chancel of the fourteenth century and a tower and chapels of the fifteenth century. There is a splendid collection of brasses, the most elaborate being the Foxley brass in the north aisle. On a column in the south aisle is a brass with an inscription, recording how a man gave up his Oxford fellowship for love. At one time a man might not marry and remain a fellow of a college. There are replicas of the brasses, for rubbing. On the north wall of the chancel is a tablet to William Goddard, who died in 1609.

North of the church is a building which in the middle ages was a chantry chapel. Since then it has been, at different times, a school, a workhouse, a prison and a drying room for eel nets. On its south wall is a little carving of a horse, which might be Norman.

The main entrance to the churchyard is through a timber-framed gatehouse built in the fifteenth century.

In the village is the Jesus Hospital, a group of 28 almshouses. It was built in 1627, under the will of William Goddard, whose statue is over the entrance and whose tablet is in the church. Frederick Walker used these almshouses as the setting for his picture 'The Harbour of Refuge', painted in 1872. It is in the Tate Gallery. Visitors may see the chapel.

Other buildings in Bray include the Georgian Chantry House, west of the church, some attractive cottages and two old inns. One of these, the Crown, is a fifteenth-century hall-house.

Bray is best known for the eighteenth-century satirical ballad about its vicar who, to keep his living, changed his religion and his politics every time there was a change of sovereign. According to the song, he survived the reigns of Charles II, James II, William and Mary, Queen Anne and George I, at the very least from 1685 to 1714. There is a problem, though, because during this time, Bray had not one vicar but three.

COOKHAM

Cookham is beside the Thames, just north of Maidenhead. To the east is Formosa Island which, at 50 acres (20 ha), is the largest island on the river.

The High Street is a happy mixture of buildings of different periods. At its west end is an open space, Cookham Moor, while at its east end it joins the A4094. On the crossroads is the Stanley Spencer Gallery (see chapter 6). Opposite are Wistaria Cottage and East Gate. When the front of Wistaria Cottage had to be rebuilt, it was done with such care that the bricks were numbered and put back in their original positions.

Turning left, the next building of interest is Tarry Stone House, of five bays and built in chequered brick. Opposite the house is the Tarry Stone itself, a sarsen which once stood on Cookham Moor. An inscription tells its story. At the entrance to the churchyard is the timber-framed Church Gate House. Finally,

we come to the elegant cast iron Cookham Bridge, built in 1867. The octagonal tollhouse on the other side was in use until 1947.

The walls of Holy Trinity Church are an attractive mixture of stone and flint. The tower is typical of Berkshire, being squat, built of flint and in the Perpendicular style. The nave is Norman, while the aisles and the arcades are thirteenth-century. Two monuments are remarkable. One, in the chancel, is to Thomas Peake, who died in 1517, and his wife. It is of Purbeck marble, with a canopy that is supported on twisted columns, and has an attractive vault inside. There is another very like it at Bisham. The second monument, on the wall of the north aisle, is a beautiful sculpture by Flaxman. It is to Sir Isaac Pococke, who was drowned in the Thames in 1810.

The church has a copy of Stanley Spencer's 'Last Supper', the original being in the gallery in the village.

Cookham is the home of the Queen's Swan Keeper, a position that has been held for many years by a member of the Turk family. One of the Keeper's duties is to conduct the Swan Upping, which takes place in July. About a hundred cygnets are 'upped' from the river and marked to show who owns them. Formerly the unfortunate birds belonged to many different institutions and had complicated patterns carved on their beaks. Now, the only people to own swans are the Queen and the Dyers' and Vintners' Companies of the City of London. The Dyers' birds have one nick on the bill, the vintners' two nicks and those of the Queen no marks at all.

Before the arrival of turkeys in England, swans were a luxury food for the privileged few, who needed to recognise the birds they owned.

EASTBURY and EAST GARSTON

Both villages are south-east of Lambourn.

At **Eastbury** the river Lambourn separates the main road and a village street. Both are lined with attractive houses. At the north-west end of the little street is Manor Farm, a brick building of the early seventeenth century. At the south-west end of the village, a few yards up the road to Eastbury Grange is a dovecote with 999 pigeon holes.

In the dovecote are the remains of the scaffolding which was used to collect the birds and which was much more convenient than an ordinary ladder. Such scaffolding swings

Cottages at East Garston.

round a central pivot, which explains why dovecotes are circular in plan.

East Garston is a delightful collection of houses and cottages, some thatched and timber-framed.

EAST ILSLEY

East Ilsley is a downland village, just east of the A34 and near the Oxfordshire border.

An old jingle says the place was:

Far famed for sheep and wool, though not for spinners,

For sportsmen, doctors, publicans and sinners.

From the seventeenth century, East Ilsley had the most important sheep fair in England, after Smithfield, as well as fortnightly markets from March to November. In the nineteenth century, when the fairs were at their height, there might be as many as eighty thousand sheep in the village at one time. The animals were offered for sale by the rearers of Wiltshire, Gloucestershire and Hampshire and from as far afield as Wales and northern England. They were bought by the graziers of Buckinghamshire and Hertfordshire, who fattened them for the London market. The fairs were still flourishing in Edwardian times, but the last one was held in 1934.

The publicans mentioned in the jingle prospered as long as the fairs did, but their number has now declined from ten to three.

The first of the sportsmen was 'Butcher' Cumberland, who defeated Bonnie Prince Charlie at Culloden in 1745. After the war he began breeding racehorses at East Ilsley. There are still several racing stables in the village.

Though the church might possibly have been founded by Canute, it is a disappointment. There are, though, two good houses, facing each other across the one-way street. Both have sash windows, showing they are late Renaissance, or classical, but one of them, by flaunting its eaves, shows that it is in the Queen Anne style, while the other, which hides its eaves behind a parapet, is Georgian.

ETON

The town of Eton is in a remarkable position. Not only is it beside the Thames and reached by a bridge designed by Telford, but it stands between Berkshire's two finest

Farnborough rectory.

monuments, Eton College and Windsor Castle (see chapter 8). The town, though, does not try to ape either of its impressive neighbours but directs its efforts to being charming and does so with great success.

The High Street is informal, being narrow and winding. It is lined with delightful old houses and shops, some timber-framed and some of brick. One curious feature is the oriel window of the Crown and Cushion, which is supported by cast iron columns. In Eton Square there is a group of former almshouses, built in the eighteenth century. The 'square' is a narrow side street leading to the right off High Street, when coming from Windsor.

FARNBOROUGH

Farnborough lies on the chalk, in the north of Berkshire.

The road through the village is lined with attractive houses. The nave and chancel of the church are of flint, but the handsome

Eton High Street

fifteenth-century tower is of ashlar, neatly squared blocks of limestone. The stone can only have come here at great expense. John Betjeman lived at Farnborough for a time, and there is a memorial window to him in the church by John Piper.

A little beyond the church, towards West Ilsley, is the delightful Georgian rectory.

HUNGERFORD
Market day, Wednesday.

Hungerford is not mentioned in Domesday Book, but a hundred years later it is referred to as a 'community of burgesses', so it may have been built as a new town. It had some distinguished lords of the manor, including several kings, Simon de Montfort and John of Gaunt.

In the seventeenth century Hungerford prospered in a modest way as a market town. Samuel Pepys came here in 1668 and ate 'very good troutes, eels and crayfish' at the Bear. In 1688 William of Orange also stayed at the Bear, where he negotiated with commissioners sent by James II.

Hungerford's golden age began with the turnpiking of the Bath Road in the eighteenth century. By 1840 the town had eight coach-ing inns. The Kennet and Avon Canal, completed in 1810, brought more prosperity and, no doubt, there were high hopes when the railway arrived in 1847. However, the railway took people away and killed much of the traffic on the roads and the canal. Hungerford became, once more, a quiet market town.

A good place to start a visit to Hungerford is at the junction of the A338 with the A4. Here is the Bear Hotel. It has a Georgian front, but it dates at least from 1494 and possibly earlier. Henry VIII settled it, with the manor of Chilton Foliat, on five of his six wives.

We now follow the A338, which is Bridge Street until it meets the Kennet and Avon Canal. Boat trips run from here (chapter 2). Next comes High Street, where there are two monstrosities, one being the railway bridge and the other the Victorian town hall. For the rest, though, High Street is delightful. As a result of several fires which destroyed the older houses, the buildings are nearly all of the eighteenth century. The most imposing is number 33. Most of the shop fronts are, alas, modern, but one old one, with its slightly bowed windows and small panes, has survived.

Hungerford High Street.

The parish church, St Lawrence's, is by the canal. The medieval church collapsed in 1814, so a new one was built using Bath stone which was brought along the new canal. The style is Gothic Revival, that is, a loose copy of the Perpendicular. The pinnacles on the tower are large enough for a building twice the size and there is a bow window at the east end, a remarkable feature for a church.

Like almost every other town and village in England, Hungerford was once administered by a manor court. Its meetings involved such dull business as the management of the common fields and, even more unpopular, the payment of dues and the election of unwilling officers. Not surprisingly, people sought to enliven these proceedings with a little merry-making. At Hungerford the court still meets to elect a Constable and ale tasters, but its members have abandoned many of the boring transactions and kept the merrymaking.

The second Tuesday after Easter is known as Tutti Day. There are two Tutti men, each carrying a 6 foot 6 inch (2 metre) Tutti pole decorated with ribbons and flowers. 'Tutti' is a dialect word for bunch of flowers. Tutti men once had the serious duty of collecting the 'head penny', a kind of poll tax, from the commoners. To sweeten every visit they had a drink with the householder, kissed his wife and made him a present of an orange. Today they forgo the penny, but everything else happens and there are a hundred homes to visit.

HURLEY

Hurley is on the Thames, just off the A423 between Maidenhead and Henley.

The village street is lined with distinguished buildings, including the Bell Inn with its sixteenth-century timber-framed front.

There used to be a priory here, but only a few fragments remain. They are the nave of the church, now the parish church, the refectory range, now part of a private house just north of the church, and two barns and a dovecote to the west of the church. One of the barns has been converted to a house. It has the dovecote in its garden. (See also chapters 2 and 4, for the river and church respectively.)

HURST

This scattered village is between Wokingham and Twyford, most of it to the west of the A321.

St Nicholas's church is mainly Victorian, though it has a Norman arcade. One of the

columns was heightened by chipping off much of its capital and building a more slender section on top of it.

The church is rich in monuments. The late sixteenth-century brasses of Richard Ward and his wife are above an older tomb-chest, cuckoos in the nest as it were. Ward was sub-treasurer from the time of Henry VIII to that of Elizabeth I, keeping his head, in both senses of the term, during four difficult reigns. The seventeenth-century monument to Lady Savile is sumptuous, and so is that of Henry Barker.

Opposite the church are some almshouses, founded by William Barker in 1664. They were for 'the maintenance of eight poor persons each at 6d *per diem* for ever'.

It is said that the bowling green beside the Castle Inn was made for the benefit of Charles II.

LAMBOURN

Lambourn is on the Berkshire Downs, in the extreme west of the county. Its people train racehorses, work on farms and make ties and Christmas crackers.

This is a village with the feel of a small town. Once it was known as Chipping (mar-

Lambourn: Ivy House.

ket) Lambourn and held three fairs a year as well as its weekly market.

There are some good Georgian houses, notably the former vicarage, south-west of the church, College House in High Street and Ivy House and number 21 in Newbury Street. One face of the Red Lion is built of sarsen stones, while there are others, unshaped, ringing the churchyard. In the wall north of the church is a doorway, ornamented with strapwork, which once led to the former manor house, Lambourn Place. Also north of the church are some pleasant almshouses grouped round a quadrangle and with an imposing entrance tower. They were founded in 1502 but rebuilt in 1852.

There are attractive cottages in Upper Lambourn.

(See also chapters 2 and 3 for Lambourn Seven Barrows, chapter 4 for the church and chapter 7 for the Lambourn Trainers Association.)

MAIDENHEAD

Maidenhead is mainly a commuter and residential town with a little light industry.

During the early middle ages Maidenhead was just a small settlement between Cookham and Bray, but the place grew after a bridge was built over the Thames in 1280. The eighteenth century was a prosperous time for the town, since it was on the Bath Road and at a convenient stopping distance from London.

There were many coaching inns, though most of them have now vanished.

It was at Maidenhead that Thomas Noel wrote his *Pauper's Drive*:

There's a grim one-horse hearse in a jolly round trot,
To the churchyard a pauper is going, I wot.
The road it is rough and the hearse has no springs
And hark to the dirge which the mad driver sings:
'Rattle his bones over the stones,
He's only a pauper that nobody owns.'

Between the two World Wars the town gained a reputation for frivolity and loose living. A road where the wealthy housed their mistresses is still known as 'Gaiety Row'.

Maidenhead has a good shopping centre, but the most attractive parts of the town are on the fringes.

Those interested in Victorian architecture should visit **Boyn Hill**, which is on the A4 towards Reading. The church, All Saints, was built in the 1850s by G. E. Street. Betjeman calls it a 'Tractarian cathedral of an upper-class suburb'. The style is of about 1300, that is between the Early English and the Decorated, but there is little resemblance to a medieval building, because Street used the most elaborate brickwork it is possible to imagine. Beside the church an archway leads to a courtyard with a vicarage, stables, school

Maidenhead Bridge, designed by Sir Robert Taylor in 1777.

Newbury: Weavers' Cottages.

and schoolmaster's house. The whole makes an impressive group and it must have been even more striking originally, when the steeple stood separate from the body of the church. But in 1911 the architect's son, A. E. Street, linked the two by adding a couple of extra bays to the nave.

To the east of the town the Thames is crossed by Sir Robert Taylor's splendid bridge of 1777, with its fine balustrade and impressive stonework. In the heyday of coaching, five hundred horses crossed it daily, drawing vehicles of many different kinds. Further south is the railway bridge by Brunel which crosses the river in just two spans, some of the widest ever built in brick. The arches look dangerously flat and the builder asked to be relieved of his contract, because he was sure that the bridge would collapse as soon as the wooden centring was removed. Luckily for him, a storm destroyed the centring just when he had finished his work, and the bridge stood. Turner painted this bridge in his 'Rain, Steam and Speed', though just as a coloured blur, so it cannot be recognised. The bridge can be reached along the Buckinghamshire bank and it is worth going to it, if only to try the echo.

Beside the A4094, towards Cookham, is Boulters' Lock, with a car park a little further on, to the left. A boulter was a miller, and there were two mills here, one of them now being a hotel. Beyond the hotel is Ray Mill Island, where there are some delightful gardens, an aviary, ducks to feed and a spectacular weir (chapter 2).

NEWBURY

Early closing, Wednesday; market day, Thursday.

Newbury is a good shopping centre and has a certain amount of light industry. It is the headquarters of the giant pharmaceutical company Bayer UK and of the prominent electronics companies Quantel and Vodaphone. Many other companies have distribution depots here because of the good road communications.

During the middle ages, and for some time after, Newbury had an important woollen industry. The most famous of the clothiers was John Smallwood, also called John Winchcombe after his place of origin, but best known as Jack of Newbury. He died in 1519. When he was asked to raise two horsemen and two footmen for Henry VIII's campaign of 1513 against the Scots, he raised fifty horse and fifty foot and marched with them himself, but they had got only as far as Stony Stratford in Buckinghamshire when they learned of the victory at Flodden.

During the Civil War two battles were fought near Newbury, one in 1643 and the other in 1644. An audio-visual display in the town's museum describes them (see chapter 6).

Following the Civil War, Newbury's cloth trade declined, but in the eighteenth century the road from London to Bath was turnpiked and, as Newbury was roughly halfway along it, the town prospered from the coach traffic. There were ten large coaching inns, of which

Lock on the Kennet and Avon Canal at Newbury.

the George and Pelican had stabling for three hundred horses. Also, in 1723 the Kennet Navigation was opened, linking Newbury to the Thames, to be followed by the Kennet and Avon Canal, which was finished in 1810. For a time Newbury was a thriving inland port.

The main line of the Great Western Railway opened in 1841. Though it did not pass through Newbury, it killed coach traffic between London and Bristol and long-distance traffic on the Kennet and Avon Canal. The opening of the branch line to Newbury in 1847 improved the town's communications but reduced the remaining local traffic on the canal. Prosperity increased again with the arrival of new industries after the Second World War.

A good place to start a visit to Newbury is at St Nicolas's church (chapter 4). From the west end of the church go along West Mills, which was once a wharf. There are several good eighteenth-century houses, especially St Nicolas House, which is not far from the church. It is of blue-grey and red brick, with aprons below the windows, and a parapet. Numbers 15-16 were once Coxedd's Almshouses, and number 18 Pearce's Almshouses. At the end, by the swing-bridge, number 22 is another fine house, this one of the Queen Anne period. In West Mills homes for the rich stand side by side with almshouses for the poor, making an interesting comment on eighteenth-century Newbury.

Cross the swing-bridge, but pause on it to admire the seventeenth-century Weavers' Cottages with their gables of various sizes.

Turn towards the town and you come to Newbury Lock, the first on the Kennet and Avon Canal. It is unusual in that the paddles, that is the sluices that let in the water, are worked by levers.

Ahead is Newbury Bridge, which once carried the road from Oxford to Southampton. It is of five spans, but only the centre one can be seen as those on either side have been buried. The bridge was built before the canal, so there is no towpath, which created a problem for the boatmen in the days of horse-drawn boats. One answer was to pass the rope across the road, whip up the horse and cast off close to the bridge. With any luck, the barge had enough momentum to carry it through, but meanwhile the rope was causing havoc among the traffic on the bridge. There is a notice by the lock forbidding this practice.

An underground passage near the bridge comes out in Northbrook Street. This street was once very fine and some of the upper storeys of the buildings are still worth seeing. The best is number 8, which dates from the 1660s. It is of brick, with pilasters and tile-hung gables. Such gables were once common in the town. Numbers 23-4 are said to be Jack of Newbury's house. The front gives no indication of its age, but the wall facing the alleyway beside it has timber framing and a fine oriel window.

Those who admire eighteenth-century

architecture should continue to the clock-tower at the end of Northbrook Street. To the left is Bath Road and to the right is London Road, both of which lay on the old turnpike that once linked the two cities. At a fork, a short distance along Bath Road, is Chestnuts, built in the early eighteenth century, but with a later doorway. Going in the opposite direction, along London Road, we come to St Mary's House, number 40. It is in grey brick, with stone surrounds to the windows. Like

Plan of Newbury, showing recommended route. Key: 1, St Nicolas's church; 2, Weavers' Cottages; 3, 8 Northbrook Street; 4, Jack of Newbury's house; 5, Chestnuts; 6, St Mary's House; 7, Market Square; 8, Newbury Museum; 9, Corn Store; 10, wharf; 11, Lower Raymonds Buildings; 12, Upper Raymonds Buildings; 13, St Bartholomew's Hospital; 14, Raymond's Almshouses.

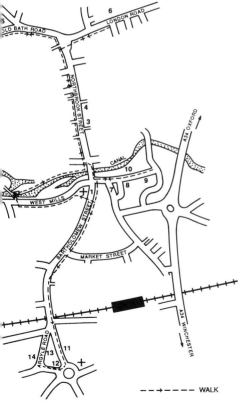

Chestnuts, it is eighteenth-century, but it makes an interesting contrast because it is Gothic Revival. This is shown by the castellated parapet and the ogee arch over the door.

Now return to Newbury Bridge, cross it and turn left into the Market Square, where the most important buildings are Victorian. The former town hall, with the clock-tower, is poor man's Gothic, the National Westminster Bank is Italian Gothic and the Corn Exchange is classical.

From the Market Square it is only a few paces to the Newbury Museum (chapter 6). Beyond the museum is a long, timber-framed building with an outside gallery, known as the Corn Store. It was once used as a warehouse for grain transported on the canal.

The open space in front of the Corn Store used to be the port of Newbury, where there were 'basons' (basins) with moorings for the large barges that plied the canal and the river. Now the basons are all filled and the only installations left are the small stone building near the bridge, once a workshop, and a restored crane, brought here from the railway goods yard.

Boat trips run from the wharf beside the old workshop.

Return now to St Nicolas's church, continue down Bartholomew Street and cross the railway into Newtown Road. On its east side are Lower Raymonds Buildings, a dignified row of classical almshouses, dated 1796. A little further along, on the other side, are Upper Raymonds Buildings, which were built in 1826 and are Gothic Revival. The two groups show, in a humbler way, the same contrast that we saw between Chestnuts and St Mary's House at the other end of the town.

Turn right at the roundabout, then right again into Argyle Road. On the right is Newbury's oldest and most distinguished charitable institution, St Bartholomew's Hospital. It was founded by King John, though the present building is seventeenth-century. It has a courtyard in front, and an imposing doorway with a cupola. 'Hospital' here means 'almshouses'.

Opposite the Hospital is a timber-framed E-shaped building, which may have been a farm in the sixteenth century but became Raymond's Almshouses in the seventeenth. In 1929 Dr Essex Wynter restored the building, adding an extra storey, but using the original materials as much as possible, though doors were brought from Eton College. It

Newbury: Bagnor Water Mill Theatre.

then became homes for retired nurses from the Middlesex Hospital. Dr Wynter also restored Bartholomew Manor House, which is also in Argyle Road, towards the town centre. Turn right out of Argyle Road into Pound Street and as you rejoin Newtown Road there is a single-storey building on the right. This is the rump of the Litten Chapel of about 1500, which once belonged to St Bartholomew's

Newbury: Falkland memorial.

Hospital, Newbury. The adjoining three-storey building was built as St Bartholomew's Grammar School in 1849.

On the northern outskirts of the town is **Shaw House**, the finest example of Elizabethan architecture in Berkshire, completed in 1581. It is not open to the public, but there is a good view of it from the road, just east of the church at OS 174: SU 475683.

A Newbury clothier, Thomas Dolman, chose to build Shaw rather than invest in his business, leading his workers to complain:

Lord have mercy on us poor sinners,
Thomas Dolman has built a new house
And has turned away all his spinners.

The house was built for show, and Dolman knew what his neighbours would feel about it. A Greek inscription over the door reads, 'Let no jealous man enter', while another, in Latin, says, 'The toothless man envies the teeth of the eater and the mole despises the eye of the deer.'

It is interesting to compare sixteenth-century Shaw with fifteenth-century Dorney Court (chapter 5). Both have high-pitched roofs, prominent chimneys and gables and large windows, some of them bays. But at Dorney Court there is delightful irregularity while at Shaw the Renaissance has disciplined these motifs in an almost perfectly symmetrical façade. Shaw also has a classical doorway.

At about 1½ miles (2.4 km) to the north-west of Newbury is the **Bagnor Water Mill Theatre** (Newbury RG16 8AE; telephone

0635 46044). Take the A4 towards Hungerford, turn on to the B4494 and look for signposts. It is an intimate little theatre with just 190 seats. It is set in lawns and gardens, beside a mill stream. There is a restaurant.

On the southern outskirts of Newbury, on the A343 towards Andover, is a Victorian memorial to Lord Falkland, who was killed at the first battle of Newbury in 1643.

Newbury has an excellent racecourse. For details of race meetings contact, Newbury Racecourse PLC, The Racecourse, Newbury (telephone: 0635 40015).

PANGBOURNE
This is a small residential town on the Thames, just west of Reading.

Pangbourne is not particularly attractive, but there are good views of the river from a pretty iron bridge and there is an excellent walk east, along the towpath.

Beside the A329 towards Oxford is a row of ornate Victorian houses known to some as the 'Seven Havens of Comfort' and to others as the 'Seven Deadly Sins'.

Church Cottage, just beside the church, is where Kenneth Grahame retired. He married rather late in life and only after he had reached the peak of his career as Secretary to the Bank of England. His wife was a masterful and eccentric woman. The couple had just one child, a son, and it was to him that Grahame told the bedtime stories which were published as *The Wind in the Willows*. The boy was blind in one eye, squinted with the other and was, moreover, timid and withdrawn. Instead of giving him the sympathy he needed, the Grahames decided he was a genius and drove him to meet their high expectations. The boy was taken away from Eton and Harrow, because he was miserable, and he was miserable, too, at Christ Church, Oxford. Eventually, he was found dead on a railway line, having, quite likely, committed suicide. Mrs Grahame sent his clothes to a jumble sale.

READING
Market days, Wednesday to Saturday.

Reading has a university, many shops and a great deal of modern industry.

The town began as a Saxon settlement on a gravel terrace between the Kennet and the Thames. The site was easy to defend and the Danes used it as a base for an attack on Wessex in AD 870, during the time of Alfred the Great.

Reading became important when Henry I founded an abbey there in 1121. The king gave it the hand of St James as a relic to attract pilgrims and, partly as a result of their offerings, it became one of the wealthiest abbeys in

Pangbourne: one of the 'Seven Deadly Sins'.

England. Parliament met in its great hall from time to time.

Like all the monasteries in England, Reading Abbey was dissolved by Henry VIII. Its abbot, Hugh of Faringdon, might have retired on a good pension, but he chose instead to oppose the king. As a result he was condemned for high treason and hanged, drawn and quartered. In 1542 the king gave Reading its Charter of Incorporation, which meant it had complete freedom to manage its own affairs. The citizens systematically wrecked the abbey buildings. Obviously they found the stone useful, but the destruction was so thorough that they must also have been inspired by hatred of their former masters, the monks.

The town changed hands several times during the Civil War, while the abbey suffered the final indignity of having the ruins of its nave blown up to improve the defences.

From the later middle ages, Reading had flourished because of its woollen industry, but in the latter part of the seventeenth century that industry declined. Prosperity returned in the eighteenth century when roads were turnpiked, the Thames was improved for barges and first the Kennet Navigation and then the Kennet and Avon Canal were opened. Numerous coaches passed through the town. Newcastle coal came up the river from London and corn and malt went back in exchange, while Bath stone was brought along the canals from the Somerset quarries.

In the nineteenth century Reading became known for its three Bs, beer, bulbs and biscuits. The second of these is something of a misnomer, since it stands for Sutton's Seeds, for whom bulbs were only a sideline. The firm was founded in 1806. It added lustre to an already good name by sending quick-growing seeds to Ireland during the potato famine of the 1840s. Sutton's are now in Torquay.

Joseph Huntley began making biscuits in Reading in 1826, to be joined in 1841 by George Palmer, who invented a stamping machine. Their products were soon world-famous. When, in 1904, the explorer Francis Younghusband made his arduous journey through Tibet and became the first European to penetrate the forbidden city of Lhasa, the Dalai Lama regaled him with a tin of Huntley and Palmer's biscuits.

Reading Extension College was founded in 1892 to take the examinations of London University. The college became a university

Plan of Reading, showing the recommended route. Key: 1, Butter Market; 2, St Laurence's church; 3, former Town Hall and museum; 4, George Hotel; 5, 39 London Road; 6, St Mary's church; 7, Vachel's Almshouses; 8, Holybrook House; 9, church of St Mary's Butts; 10, former McIlroy's building; 11, Abbey Gatehouse; 12, Blake's Lock Museum.

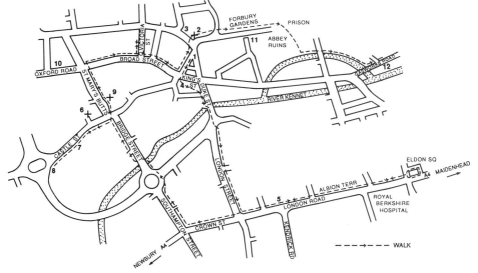

Left: *Reading: 39 London Road, home of Mary Russell Mitford.*
Right: *Reading: the Maiwand Lion in Forbury Gardens.*

in its own right in 1925.

Unfortunately, what impresses most during a visit to Reading is the powers of destruction which its people have shown over the centuries, each generation obliterating much of what it inherited. There is, though, enough left to trace the history of the town in its buildings.

A good place to start a tour of Reading is the triangular Butter Market.

At the northern apex of the triangle is St Laurence's church. It was founded in 1121, the same year as the abbey, but little of the original Norman work remains. Much of the building dates from the fifteenth and sixteenth centuries, including the tower with its polygonal buttresses, the arcade and the roofs. All this later work is in the Perpendicular style.

On the south wall of the nave is a monument to John Blagrave, a mathematician who died in 1611. Surrounding it are figures representing the five regular geometric solids, the icosahedron, the dodecahedron, the octahedron, the tetrahedron and the cube.

Behind St Laurence's is the former Town Hall, built by Alfred Waterhouse in 1875 (chapter 6).

If we include the church, every period in the history of Reading is represented in the little market place. On the west side is a timber-framed house of the sixteenth or seventeenth century; in the south-east corner is a Georgian house; on the west side again is the former Corn Exchange of 1854; finally, there is a sprinkling of modern buildings.

In the centre of the triangle is an elegant stone lamp standard of 1804 given by Edward Simeon 'as a mark of affection to his native town' and designed by Sir John Soane. Almost touching it is the exhaust flue of a public lavatory.

In King Street, and close to the market place, is the sixteenth-century George Hotel, with its attractive courtyard.

Duke Street crosses the Kennet by a small but elegant stone bridge of 1788 and leads to a stream of traffic, beyond which is London Street. In 1949 Betjeman described this as 'the handsomest street in Reading', but its Georgian houses are now unfortunately decayed.

At the far end of London Street, turn left into London Road. Here are Reading's finest Georgian buildings. Opposite Kendrick Road is number 39, an attractive brick house which was the childhood home of the authoress Mary Russell Mitford (see under Three Mile Cross). Next there are some Georgian terraces on both sides of the road. The most impressive is Albion Terrace, which has iron balconies, showing that it is Regency, that is early nineteenth-century.

The central block of the Royal Berkshire Hospital dates from the 1830s. It is in Bath stone, brought here along the Kennet and Avon Canal. The Victorians added a great deal to the original block, but their work is in harmony with it.

Reading: Holybrook House, Castle Street.

The Italianate villas of Eldon Square are early Victorian.

Castle Street begins with some timber-framed and early Georgian houses. St Mary's church, with its classical front, was once a Congregational chapel. Vachel's Almshouses, at right angles to the street, were founded in 1634 and endowed with £40 a year 'for ever'. They were rebuilt in 1864. Holybrook House, which faces the roundabout, has a magnificent door case with heavily blocked columns and a fearsome keystone.

The church of St Mary in St Mary's Butts has an attractive tower of 1550 with a chequerboard pattern of stone blocks and flint panels. The south arcade of about 1200 is late Norman in style.

At the end of St Mary's Butts, glance along Oxford Road to see the former McIlroy's building. It was by Frank Morris. There is much of his work hereabouts, notably in Queen Victoria Street. Morris favoured ginger-coloured stone, public lavatory bricks and exuberant ornament.

Return to the Butter Market and take the path on the north side of the church. The flint building to the left was once the guest house of the abbey. The path leads to Forbury Gardens, which are very pleasant. The gardens are dominated by the Maiwand Lion, which commemorates the men of the Berkshire Regiment who died in the Afghan campaign of 1879-80. South of the gardens is the Abbey Gatehouse, rebuilt by Gilbert Scott in 1861. The upstairs room was once a school, whose pupils included Jane Austen.

An underpass leads from the gardens to the abbey ruins. They are mere fragments and have been stripped of their facing stones so that only the rubble core remains. First comes the south transept of the church, which had two chapels to the east, semi-circular in plan. Next comes the slype, a passageway that linked the cloister to the monastery gardens and the cemetery. Adjoining the slype is the chapter house, with an apsidal end. Running south from here is a length of wall, all that remains of the dormitory, and at right angles to it is the reredorter, or lavatory.

Britain's first round or canon for four voices, 'Sumer is icumen in', was composed at Reading Abbey in the thirteenth century.

East of the ruins is the prison, where Oscar Wilde served his sentence and where he composed the *Ballad of Reading Gaol.* A path beside it leads to Chestnut Walk and so to Gasworks Road and Blake's Lock Museum (chapter 6). From the museum there is a good view of the prison.

The Museum of English Rural Life at Whiteknights is described in chapter 6.

SLOUGH

In 1900 Slough was an insignificant place, with a population of about 7000. Then, in 1920, a company called Slough Estates bought 700 acres (283 ha) of land and created something which was then quite new, a trading estate. Today, the estate has eight hundred factories and the town's population is close on 100,000. Mars UK, the chocolate manufacturer, is one of the many important companies based here.

Anyone who studies modern industrial architecture will find much of interest, while there are many excellent amenities, such as sports centres and swimming pools, a good shopping centre and 600 acres (242 ha) of attractive parkland. There are all kinds of sports, including American football.

Queen Victoria made her first railway journey in 1842 and it was from Slough that she took the train. She did not, though, use the existing station, which dates from 1882. This remarkable building has a large central pavilion flanked by smaller ones, while the roof gives it a French look.

One of Slough's few antiquities is the Montem Mound, which is in Montem Lane, near the Montem Sports Centre. It looks like a nondescript pile of earth, damaged, moreover, by people climbing on it, but is certainly very old. No one knows for certain what it is. Though about the right size for a burial mound, it is not the same shape as any prehistoric barrow. Until the middle of the nineteenth century Eton College held a ceremony here, every year. The sovereign attended and, along with others, was expected to give 'salt', or money, which helped pay the expenses of

Eton boys at Cambridge. This part of Slough is still known as Salt Hill.

It is possible that Eton had appropriated a local festivity which might have begun in pagan times.

The astronomer Sir William Herschel (1738-1822), who discovered the planet Uranus, lived and worked at Slough.

The church at Langley Marish is described in chapter 4 and Slough Museum in chapter 6.

SONNING

Sonning (pronounced Sunning) is beside the Thames, to the north-east of Reading. It is most attractive but draws so many visitors that it is best avoided on Sundays and public holidays.

The church contains a great deal of medieval work but has been so heavily restored that most of it looks Victorian. It has a good collection of tombs, particularly remarkable being the seventeenth-century Rich monument, under the tower. Four putti, or little boys, support an enormous slab of black marble on which stand two white urns. In 1853 the *Ecclesiologist* described this tomb as 'the vilest paganism imaginable'. On the floor near the font is a brass to a judge, Lord Stowell, who died in 1836. He was courting the Dowager Duchess of Sligo when her son was brought

Sonning: Turpin's, the house once owned by Dick Turpin's aunt.

before him for enticing two men to desert from the Navy. Stowell jailed the son and, three months later, married the mother.

South of the church is a long brick wall, beyond which there was once a palace belonging to the Bishops of Sarum, or Salisbury. Earlier, in Anglo-Saxon times, the Bishop of Ramsbury in Wiltshire was sometimes based in Sonning and known then as the Bishop of Sonning. In 1399, when Richard II was deposed, his child wife Isabella was brought here to be protected by the bishop. Her ghost is said to haunt the paths by the river.

The main streets of the village form a capital A with the point towards the east, away from the river. The left-hand stroke is Thames Street, the right hand stroke is Pearson Street while the High Street forms part of the cross stroke. Walking along Pearson Street from the east, we come to the Robert Palmer Cottages of 1850, which are almshouses. Then, after several attractive houses and cottages, comes The Grove, facing down High Street. It has three gables, which is odd, as it is early eighteenth-century, by which time gables were out of fashion. Over the doorway is a canopy with some excellent pendants. Admiral Villeneuve stayed here after he had been captured at Trafalgar, and General Eisenhower used the place as a weekend retreat during the Second World War. At the west end of the street is Turpin's, which belonged to the aunt of Dick Turpin, the highwayman, who sometimes took refuge here.

High Street has a pleasant medley of houses of different periods and styles. At the bottom, a turning leads to the timber-framed Bull Inn. A steep slope links High Street to Thames Street and on the left of it, but well hidden, is Deanery Gardens by Edwin Lutyens. The house has a weathervane of a parson preaching to empty chairs.

Thames Street leads to the river, which is especially attractive here, with several weeping willows. There is a handsome brick eighteenth-century bridge and, just the other side of it in Oxfordshire, is an old mill which is now a restaurant and theatre combined (telephone: 0734 698000).

STREATLEY

The village is beside the Thames, in the Goring Gap. In High Street, which leads towards the river and Goring, is Streatley House, Georgian, of five bays and three storeys.

The church has a fifteenth-century tower, but all the rest is Victorian.

From the bridge there is a good view of the river. The ornamental barge moored by the hotel once belonged to Magdalen College, Oxford (see front cover).

It is possible to reach the riverbank by taking the path beside the church, then keeping to the right.

THREE MILE CROSS

Three Mile Cross is to the south of Reading, close to Junction 11 of the M4. It has but one building of interest, the home of the authoress Mary Russell Mitford. It is opposite two garages and next to the Bull Inn (OS 175: SU 716679).

Mary Mitford was born in 1787. When she was ten her father bought her a lottery ticket which won her £20,000, but he kept the money for himself and by 1820 had spent it all. Until then the family had lived in a handsome house in Reading (see entry for the town), but they now moved to Three Mile Cross, where the father became the village doctor. In 1819 Mary wrote an article on the village for *The Lady Magazine*. The article was a success, so more followed, and eventually they were all published together as *Our Village*, one of the most delightful books ever written on the English countryside. Dr Mitford spent the royalties from it and from Mary's later works. He died in 1842, leaving his daughter in debt, but her books were so popular that there was a public subscription which paid all she owed. She died at Swallowfield (chapter 5) in 1851.

WALTHAM ST LAWRENCE

Waltham St Lawrence is between Reading and Maidenhead. It is one of the most attractive villages in Berkshire.

The church seems to have been a short Norman building since two bays of the nave belong to that period, but in the early fourteenth century two more bays were added to the east. The tower was built at the same time, though it has a fifteenth-century door and a brick top of uncertain date.

Close to the church is the fourteenth-century Bell Inn, which has a magnificent timber frame. A post-and-rail fence and four ash trees have replaced the village pound in the middle of the green.

On the left, as you walk away from the church, is Ivy Bank Farm with its five gables.

Waltham St Lawrence: the Bell Inn.

The roughcast may be hiding a timber frame. At the far end of the street, Coltman's and Kellingham's are two impressive houses, both of about 1600. Paradise House, which faces the war memorial, is Georgian and, unusually for its period, is irregular in shape.

WARGRAVE

Wargrave is on the Thames, between Twyford and Henley.

The centre of the village is a crossroads from which High Street runs north, towards Henley. A short distance along it, on the left, is Woodclyffe Hall of 1902, which was paid for by a local philanthropist, inspired by Norman Shaw and designed by Cole Adams. It has an oriel characteristic of Shaw. Further along, and again on the left, is Barrymore, which in the late eighteenth century belonged to an Irish peer, the Earl of Barrymore. He ruined himself by building and maintaining a theatre in the village. At the end of High Street is the St George and Dragon, one of Jerome K. Jerome's favourite pubs. Hanging in the restaurant is its former sign, which was painted by two members of the Royal Academy, G. D. Leslie and J. Hodgson.

In Church Street, which runs west from the central crossroads, is Woodclyffe Hostel, now a public library. It is also by Cole Adams.

The church is in an attractive park, with chestnut trees. It has a tower of 1635, but the rest is quite new. In 1914 suffragettes burnt the original building because the vicar refused to omit the word 'obey' from the wedding ceremony.

Wargrave: the Hannen Mausoleum by Lutyens in the churchyard.

Telford's iron bridge over the Thames at Windsor.

WINDSOR

Market day, Saturday.

The old town of Windsor grew up under the walls of the castle. It is a compact group of little streets on the south side of the castle, opposite the main entrance. Among them is Queen Charlotte Street, which, at 51 feet 10 inches (15.8 metres), claims to be the shortest in England. Here are many delightful old houses, some timber-framed and some with Georgian shop fronts. At the corner of Church Lane and St Alban's Street is the former free school, a brick building of the late seventeenth century. The front facing St Alban's Street has a pediment across its full width and, curiously, an arch joining two chimneys. The Three Tuns, at the other end of Church Lane, was built in 1518 as the Guildhall of Holy Trinity. In medieval times people formed such guilds to help each other in time of need and to pray for the souls of departed members.

In contrast with this network of little alleys, High Street, which runs beside it, is wide and impressive. Here is the Guildhall of 1690, designed by Sir Thomas Fitch, but completed after his death by Sir Christopher Wren. It has an open ground floor for market stalls, with council chambers above. The council, not wishing to fall through the floor, insisted on extra columns in the middle of the space below. Wren said they were not necessary and, to prove his point, made them so that they did not quite touch the ceiling. On the north face of the Guildhall is a statue of Queen Anne and on the opposite side is one of her consort, Prince George of Denmark. The Guildhall, a Grade I listed building, has been superbly adapted to become a conference and banqueting centre. Features include two solid brass chandeliers, on loan from the Queen, each weighing $6\frac{1}{4}$ cwt (317 kg). For further information contact Windsor Guildhall, High Street, Windsor SL4 1LR; telephone: 0628 796033, 796013 or 798888.

A little further along High Street, away from the castle, is St John the Baptist's church. This was built in the 1820s, so the style is Gothic Revival. The tower, like the one at Hungerford, has oversize pinnacles. During the early nineteenth century pioneer work was being done in the use of iron in buildings, and the architect of St John's, Charles Hollis, put slender cast iron columns in its arcades. The ceiling, too, is iron. On two sides of the south

74

chapel are railings carved by Grinling Gibbons.

The other buildings in High Street are a mixture of Georgian and Victorian, most of them attractive.

After High Street comes Park Street, which is entirely Georgian, numbers 12-16 and 23-4 being particularly good. The street ends with Jeffry Wyatville's gates to the Home Park. From here, Broad Walk runs for 2^{1}/2 miles (4 km) in a straight line to the Copper Horse, an equestrian statue of George III (chapter 5). Frogmore House is tantalisingly close, but it cannot be reached from Broad Walk (for instructions see chapter 8). On three days in May each year, however, signposts point the way to the Royal Mausoleum in Frogmore Gardens where Queen Victoria and Prince Albert are buried. A mausoleum had already been built here for the Duchess of Kent, the Queen's mother, when Albert died in 1861; the larger, Romanesque building beside it, with much Italian High Renaissance decoration and marble monuments, was completed in 1872. For information ring 0753 868286.

In Sheet Street, and facing down Victoria Street, is Hadleigh House, a fine building of the late eighteenth century. It is five bays wide and two and a half storeys high with a good doorway and attractive iron gates. The house's surroundings are unworthy of it.

In Victoria Street are the Windsor Almshouses of 1862. They are of yellow and red brick and, with their steep gables and dormer windows, are a good example of exuberant Victorian Gothic. In contrast, King's Road has terraces of the early nineteenth century which are classical, restrained and elegant.

Thames Street runs from the other end of High Street. First comes the White Hart Hotel, which Betjeman called 'a late Victorian disaster', and this is followed, as the street bends, by a terrace of what were fine Georgian buildings until they were ruined by plate-glass shop windows. Towards the bottom, on the right, is a memorial to Prince Christian Victor, a grandson of Queen Victoria who was killed in 1900, fighting in the Boer War. At the corner with Datchet Road is Lutyens's memorial to George V. On seeing it, the visitor's first reaction may well be to wonder what has become of the king. But he is represented by his regalia, the clothes without their emperor, as it were.

From this crossroads a street for pedestrians leads past a house where Wren once lived and on to Telford's iron bridge over the Thames, linking Windsor with Eton.

A short distance along Datchet Road, the classical building in yellow brick, on the right, is St George's School. This is the choir school of St George's Chapel.

Beyond Riverside Station, on the left, an avenue of trees runs beside a section of the Home Park which is always open to the public. From here it is possible to reach the river and walk along the towpath, past Romney Lock to Datchet. The total distance is just under 2 miles (3 km). Those wishing to go all the way to Datchet must cross the river by the Victoria Bridge.

For another walk by the Thames, go down River Street and turn left, taking either the Esplanade or Barry Avenue. In just over half a mile (800 metres), a tunnel under the Windsor and Eton relief road leads to **Clewer**. St Andrew's church here is of flint with a squat west tower and a shingle-covered spire. There is much Norman work, especially the south arcade, and there is a splendid Norman font, decorated with arches, leaves and a zigzag frieze.

Windsor has a good racecourse. For information contact Windsor Racing Limited, The Racecourse, Maidenhead Road, Windsor (telephone: 0753 865234 and 864726).

Windsor Castle is described in chapter 8. See also chapters 6 and 7.

WOKINGHAM

This is a residential town, but with a little light industry.

The centre of Wokingham is a triangular market place and on it is an amusing Victorian town hall, also triangular. From here there are two streets that are worth exploring. One is Rose Street, which is quiet and is lined with modest but picturesque houses, some timber-framed and some brick. Formerly there was an inn here called the Rose, where Gay, Pope and Swift spent a rainy day composing verses to 'sweet Molly Meg', the innkeeper's lovely daughter.

At the far end Rose Street narrows and the parish church, All Saints, is framed in the gap. This church has been heavily restored but the tower, arcade, clerestory and roof are all medieval. Just inside the churchyard, on the left, is a monument to Sir Thomas Beaver, which has a lengthy and interesting inscription.

Broad Street, which also leads from the

market place, is wide, busy and imposing. There are many fine buildings, the best of them being The Elms. It is Georgian, with a central block of five bays and two lower wings, each of one bay. At the far end, facing down the street, is the timber-framed Tudor House. From here the left fork is Shute End, with still more Georgian houses. Those of The Terrace look particularly well, standing on their grassy bank.

Wokingham's best building is the Lucas Hospital, a group of seventeenth-century almshouses. It is 2 miles (3 km) from the town centre, at the end of Luckley Road, which is off the A321 towards Sandhurst. Take the second turning on the left after the second railway bridge. Visitors should make an appointment with the matron (telephone: 0734 781443).

YATTENDON

Yattendon is 6 or 7 miles (10-11 km) northeast of Newbury.

John Norreys died here in 1597. His grandfather was executed by Henry VIII for alleged adultery with Anne Boleyn, but that did not prevent John from becoming one of the leading soldiers of the daughter of Henry and Anne, Elizabeth I.

There is a tablet in the church describing John's exploits, but, with great tact, it does not mention an unsuccessful expedition to Portugal which he and Drake led in 1589.

In 1876 the manor came to the architect Alfred Waterhouse. Waterhouse's daughter married the poet Robert Bridges, who became precentor at the church. He and Professor H. Ellis Wooldridge edited the *Yattendon Hymnal*, hoping to revive old tunes

Left: *Wokingham: the town hall.*
Right: *Wokingham: Rose Street and the church.*

Yattendon: the former reading room.

that were in danger of being forgotten. A tablet in the church commemorates Bridges, his wife and his mother, but the poet, at his own request, had no tomb. His ashes were scattered in the graveyard.

Yattendon's buildings show what a patriarchal lord of the manor might do for his tenants. Waterhouse cared for his people's souls, minds and bodies, in that order of importance. He thoroughly restored the church, he built a school, where religion would have been an important subject, he built a reading room and he built a well house. Mrs Waterhouse taught the villagers how to make copper utensils and opened a shop in London to sell them. The church still has a font ewer from that time. Yattendon copper became well known and widely sold. The Church of the Ascension at Cala in South Africa has a lectern from the village.

The centre of Yattendon is a triangular open space. On one side are shops and a pub; on another side are more shops; on the third side is Waterhouse's reading room, now a private house. Waterhouse's well house, which today is a bus shelter, is in the middle of the triangle.

The church was so heavily restored that it looks Victorian, but the structure dates from 1450 apart from the vestry and porch. The rood screen was restored under Waterhouse's supervision, incorporating medieval with new work. The choir stalls were designed and given by Paul Waterhouse. The pulpit is Jacobean.

East of the church are two Georgian houses, the Rectory, which is classical, and the Malthouse, which has a Gothic look. Further east again is Alfred Waterhouse's school, with its delightful little spire.

10
Tourist information centres

Bracknell: Central Library, Town Square, Bracknell RG12 1BH. Telephone: 0344 423149.
Maidenhead: The Library, St Ives Road, Maidenhead SL6 1QY. Telephone: 0628 781110.
Newbury: The Wharf, Newbury RG14 5AS. Telephone: 0635 30267.
Reading: Town Hall, Blagrave Street, Reading RG1 1QH. Telephone: 0734 566226.
Windsor: Central Station, Thames Street, Windsor SL4 1PJ. Telephone: 0753 852010.

BERKSHIRE

Grim's Ditch

Ridgeway

Lambourn
Seven Barrows

+ Great Fawley

Farnborough

East Ilsley

Streatley

R. Tham

Aldworth

Basildon Park

O+■ Lambourn

Eastbury

East Garston

Hampstead Norreys +

+ Ashampstead

Beale Bird Park

Pangbour

+ Great Shefford

Yattendon

Tidmars

M4

14

13

Grimsbury Castle

Bradfield ■

Eng Hou

Wickham +

Boxford

Snelsmore Common

Bucklebury +

Sole Common Pond

Donnington Castle

Bucklebury Common

Sulhams

Avington

Thatcham Moor

+ Douai Abbey

HUNGERFORD

Kennet and Avon Canal

+ M ■
NEWBURY

Padworth +

Inkpen Common

Enborne

Aldermaston ■

Grim's Bank

Wasing +

Grim's Bank

Inkpen Beacon

Walbury Hill

Silcheste

Cock
Marsh

+ Bisham   M■
Cookham

Remenham *   *+■ Hurley
Robin Hood's   Boulters'
Arbour   Lock *
Maidenhead Thicket *   MAIDENHEAD
Courage Shire O   ■
Horse Centre   A423(M) Bray ■
Wargrave   Shottesbrooke   8/9   Dorney ▲Court
Waltham ■   +   Monkey
St Lawrence   Island
tbury Farm ,•   O Thames
yard   Valley
Vineyard
READING M■   Dinton Pastures   Winkfield
Sonning   ■   Country Park   Hurst   Warfield +   +   + Cranbourne
A329(M)   10   Windsor
M4   A329(M)   Binfield ■   Great Park *▲
Bearwood   BRACKNELL   Ascot
11   ▲College   ■   ■
■ Three Mile   WOKINGHAM   + Easthampstead
Cross
Arborfield   California   Caesar's   The
Swallowfield ▲   M   Country Park   Camp ⊓   * Look Out
Park   * Crowthorne
Finchampstead   *   Wood
Ridges *   Simon's
▲   M *   Wellington   Wood
Stratfield   Country Park
Saye House

7   SLOUGH
Dorney   6 M■
Eton   + Langley
M▲   Marish
MO■▲   M4
WINDSOR   5
O
Windsor Safari   Queen Mother
Park   Reservoir

Magna Carta
Island
R. Thames

Savill Garden
▲
▲ Valley Gardens

KEY

* Countryside (Ch. 2)
⊓ Place of archaeological interest (Ch. 3)
+ Church (Ch. 4)
▲ Historic building or garden (Ch. 5 and 8)
M Museum (Ch. 6)
O Other place to visit (Ch. 7)
■ Town or village (Ch. 9)

Index